The
CELTIC
SAINTS

D1413223

d 00

The
CELTIC
SAINTS

AN ILLUSTRATED AND
AUTHORITATIVE GUIDE TO
THESE EXTRAORDINARY
MEN AND WOMEN

NIGEL PENNICK

Sterling Publishing Co., Inc.
New York

Designed and produced by
BRIDGEWATER BOOK COMPANY LTD

Picture research by Vanessa Fletcher

The publishers would like to thank the
following for use of pictures:
The Bridgeman Art Library, e.t. archive,
Fine Art Photographic Library Ltd.,
Fortean Picture Library, Sonia Halliday &
Laura Lushington, Caitlin Matthews.

Library of Congress Cataloging-in-Publication
Data Available

1 3 5 7 9 10 8 6 4 2

Published 1997 by Sterling Publishing Company, Inc.
387 Park Avenue South, New York, N.Y. 10016

Originally published in Great Britain
in 1997 by Thorsons

© 1997 Godsfield Press

Text © 1997 Nigel Pennick

Illustration © 1997 Lorraine Harrison

Distributed in Canada by Sterling Publishing
c/o Canadian Manda Group, One Atlantic Avenue,
Suite 105, Toronto, Ontario, Canada M6K 3E7

Printed in Hong Kong

Sterling HB ISBN 0-8069-9600-5
Sterling PB ISBN 0-8069-9601-3

CONTENTS

ABOVE: King Edgar adoring Christ and the angels. St.
Cuthbert and Etheldrida, abbess of Ely, accompany the king.

Introduction

"The three principal endeavours of a Bard:
One is to learn and collect sciences.
The second is to teach.
And the third is to make peace
and to put an end to all injury;
for to do contrary to these things
is not usual or becoming to a Bard."

THE TRIADS OF BRITAIN

❧

Although they are highly respected in the Christian tradition, technically the Celtic saints are not saints in the Catholic meaning of the word. Catholic saints are pious men and women recognized as exceptional by popes, and canonized with the epithet sanctus or "holy." The Celtic saints were never made so by Roman popes, but by popular veneration. Holy men and women have always played an important role in Celtic society, from pre-Christian times until the present day. To pagan and Christian Celts alike, religion was never distinct from the activities of every-day life. The old Celtic paganism was essentially nature-venerating and polytheistic, recognizing goddesses as well as gods. These could, and did, appear anywhere and everywhere in nature, as trees,

ST. SAMSON

ST. BRIGID

ST. PATRICK

animals or within natural forces and processes. Then, the Druids understood the course of nature as a manifestation of the will of the gods and goddesses. They venerated both local and general deities, which they saw as dwelling in natural sanctuaries, especially in ensouled places in the landscape. So their main places of worship were on holy hills, by springs, rivers, lakes, trees, and in certain woods. Pagan Celtic spirituality asserted the cyclic nature of exis-tence, and envisaged an immediate continuity between this material world and otherworldly realms. Recorded Druidic teachings speak of an integrated relationship between humans and nature. Traditional Celtic culture is integrated with nature, expressed through the multiple possibilities of life itself. Most of this customary lore is preserved in Celtic folk tradition.

The Celtic Christian church did not view things very differently. According to the Welsh bard, the Reverend J. Williams ab Ithel, "The Bards believed that all things were tending to

ST. DAVID

perfection; when, therefore, they embraced Christianity, they must on their own principles have viewed it as a stage in advance of their former creed." There was a genuine continuity and not a complete break that marked the transition from pagan to Christian. Of course, all of nature now was seen as the handiwork of God rather than something infused with divine power in its own right. But in Celtic Christianity, as before, it was still understood that there is an unseen world interpenetrating the visible world. Only the interpretation had changed. Everything exists on several simultaneous levels: human consciousness interprets them as the physical, the spiritual, and the symbolic, that are all various aspects of God's creation.

Celtic tradition recognizes perhaps thousands of individual saints. Some, such as St. Brigid and St. Patrick, are of international fame, others, like St. David and St. Columba, are national figures, while the majority are local and less well known. Attached to the vast majority are stories, legends, and fables which range from more or less factual accounts of the saint's life to events with a mythological dimension. The function of these stories, in socio-religious terms, is independent of the truth or falsity that we may ascribe to them. Their place in Celtic Christian culture is effective, whether or not the saints existed historically as individual human beings, and whether their legends are symbolic or factual. In this book, I do not intend to pass judgment upon the scientific objective reality of the saints and their acts, nor upon the truth or validity of the theologies that they imply. The very fact that their stories have been handed on from generation to generation for up to 1,500 years is evidence enough that they are valuable.

Although traditionally their lives are held to be paragons of Christian virtue, many of the more significant Celtic saints actually assimilated the archetypal qualities of the older gods, goddesses, and elemental beings.

ST. ANNE

St. Anna, for instance, who also appears in Celtic legend as St. Non, has the attributes of the goddess Anna or Dana, mother of the gods, and ancestress of Celtic nobility. The Welsh St. Beuno, who resurrected a number of slain young women, and made the land fertile for fruit trees and cattle, like the Scottish St. Maelrubha, was honored with cattle sacrifices until quite recently. Other Celtic saints are less archetypal and more historic, such as St. Patrick, who brought the Christian religion to Ireland, and St. Teilo, founder of many churches in south Wales.

ST. CUTHBERT

Until recent times, many Celtic saints were worshiped in Wales, Scotland, Ireland, and Brittany in the same manner as their pagan forerunners whom they supplanted. In the medieval era these traditions were prevalent, but wherever Protestantism was successful, they were eliminated. At Llanderfel in Merionethshire, Wales, the image of the god or saint called Darvel Gadarn was reported in 1538 to be something "in which the people have so greate confidence, hope and trust, that they come dayly a pilgrimage unto hym, some with kyne, other with oxen and horses." In an attempt to stop local reverence for this saint, his image was taken to London and publicly burned at Smithfield in the same year. In 1589, John Ansters reported that at St. Beuno's church at Clynog on the Lleyn peninsula in north Wales, bulls bearing a certain mark were being sacrificed "the half to God and to Beuno." Like the veneration of St. Gwen Teirbron, this custom also dwindled away in the nineteenth century.

Although, in Britain, all saints, Celtic or not, are called "saint," in contemporary Ireland, a distinction is made between Celtic and Catholic saints. Before the names of non-Irish saints, the epithet san is used, while for Celtic saints, and biblical saints, the word naomh "blessed" precedes their name. In this book, following British tradition, and in recognition that they were all holy men and women, the epithet "saint" is used for all of them.

Where the Saints Lived

The majority of the Celtic saints were revered throughout Wales, Scotland, Ireland, and Brittany. Some, however, led peripatetic lives as missionaries, traveling across the countryside, converting the pagan population to Christianity. St. Aidan, for example, traveled from Iona in the Western Isles of Scotland to Lindisfarne, an island on the Northumbrian coast where he was succeeded by St. Cuthbert, whose body eventually came to rest at Durham.

LINDISFARNE

DURHAM

WHITBY

BUXTON

LLANRHAIADR
HOLYWELL
LLANDRILLO-
YN-RHOS
GWYTHERIN
LLANDEGLA
LLANGOLLEN
PUFFIN
ISLAND
GLYNNOG FAWR
ANGLESEY

GLASGOW

LOCH
MAREE

IONA

DOWN
PATRICK

BANGOR

LONDONDERRY

ARMAGH

KELLS

MEATH

KILDARE

DURROW

KILMORE

ST. NEOTS

LLANBADARN
FAWR

NEVERN LLANDEGLEY

LYDNEY

GLAMORGAN

PENALLY

LLANTWIT MAJOR

BATH

CARHAMPTON

ALTARNON

TINTAGEL

ROCHE

PADSTOW

GULVAL

VOSGES

MORBIHAN

The
CELTIC
SAINTS

The World of the Celtic Saints

The lives and acts of the Celtic saints cannot be understood without first looking at the world in which they lived. Southern Britain was part of the western Roman Empire until the early part of the fifth century. Britain had been invaded by Rome in the year 43, the beginning of a war of conquest that led to the subjection of much of the island to Roman rule. A new infrastructure, based upon excellent roads and cities, transformed the level of civilization in a few years. Roman religion was polytheistic, the most important deities including Jupiter, Venus, Mars, Minerva, Mercury, Diana, Saturn, Victoria, Vulcan, Neptune, Ceres, Apollo, and Pluto. An important Roman idea adopted in Britain was the *Interpretatio Romana*, in which native goddesses and gods were assimilated into the framework of the newly accepted Roman religion. Thus, the Celtic pantheon was reasserted under Roman patronage. So, Teutates, the god of the clan, became identified with Mars, as were the gods of war and defence, Belutocadros and Cocidius. Sul, the goddess of the hot springs at Bath, was assimilated with the Roman goddess, Minerva, while Rosmerta became the consort of Mercury. Local divinities of holy stones, wells, rivers, and trees were acknowledged either under their Celtic names, or through the *Interpretatio Romana*.

Alongside the worship of deities in the Roman pantheon, and dead heroes elevated to divinity, there was the official cult of the spirit of the emperor. For many this cult was the most contentious religious issue, being the cause of the persecution of Druids, Jews, and Christians who could not pay the obligatory homage before the emperor's image. In addition to the official cults of Roman religion, and their Celtic counterparts, there were a number of ethnic and mystery religions in Roman Britain. It is also likely that there were Jews, worshiping according to their religious beliefs. The mystery religions included the veneration of the Egyptian goddess, Isis, in her Hellennic aspect as Isis Panthea, the personification of all goddesses. This religion was important in Britain, as attested by the largest temple of Isis north of the Alps that stood in Roman London. There was also the fertility cult of Cybele, the great mother goddess of Asia Minor; the sky-god mysteries of Jupiter Dolichenus; the ecstatic religion of Dionysus; the soldiers' patriarchal initiatory cultus of Mithras, and the Christian faith, which also excluded women from the priesthood. Several of these religions approached monotheism, either overtly or practically.

LEFT: The Virgin and Child, St. Barbara and St. Bridget depicted in the stained glass window of Storminster Newton Church, Dorset.

Although Druidism had been extirpated in southern Britain by the Romans in the year 61, by the end of Roman rule in Britain, the Celtic priesthood still flourished to the south in Gaul, to the west in Ireland and to the north among the Picts. It is likely that, once Roman rule had ended, Druidic traditions were re-established in the former colony, that had once been the center of the religion. The disintegration of Roman rule was accompanied by invasions of Picts in the north, Irish in the west, Angles, Saxons, and Jutes in the east and south. Religiously, some of the Romano-British were Christian, whilst others remained faithful to paganism.

The Romanized Britons who remained after the withdrawal of the legions were divided on ethnic lines. Those who were members of Roman families, or considered themselves still to be Roman, appear to have been largely Christian. They continued to speak Latin, and attempted to retain their Roman customs, traditions, and institutions. The genealogies of the British saints who founded or reestablished Christianity in Britain after the withdrawal of the legions show that they were all members of one or other of the noble families of Britain. The others, who saw themselves ethnically as Britons, reestablished their Celtic language and customs, and remained pagan. This polarization of the populace is typical of post-colonial countries, and it has happened many times in recent history, often leading to bitter and protracted civil wars. However, by necessity, the Christian faction in Britain also cut their ties with the Roman Empire, and from their numbers came the priests who would be the founders of the Celtic church. The Christian British saw themselves as the guardians of Christian civilization against the invaders, who were all worshipers of other deities. It is this view that underlies the medieval Arthurian romances, based ultimately upon this historical period, known as The Wasting of Britain. We will come to this in the next chapter. It was these missionaries of the Celtic church, who worked among the pagan Britons and eventually converted them, who were remembered as the Celtic saints.

ABOVE: Berec, the Briton stands up to the Romans.

The Transition from Paganism to Christianity

As the years passed, the Celtic ancestral holy places were altered gradually by Christian worship. Aspects of Celtic paganism that were not unacceptable to the new religion were absorbed, while other elements were discouraged. The local legends of the old gods, goddesses and heroes were gradually reworked as episodes from the lives of Christian saints. Thus, the new religion did not disrupt traditional society, but maintained its continuity and hence its stability. The main change from paganism to Christianity came from the new exclusion of women from most of their traditional religious roles. In the Christian church, there was no place for priestesses or seeresses. Nuns were strictly subordinate to male priests, and only exceptional women, like St. Brigid and St. Hilda, could rise to positions of influence. On occasion, women were actually expelled from their traditional places, as when St. Columba deported all cows and women from the holy isle of Iona.

As archetypal qualities, spiritual essences are implicit rather than explicit in the material world. However, they are real: thoughts, ideas, physical objects, happenings, and places can be interpreted in terms of these essences. When, occasionally, an individual human being approaches one of these archetypes in her or his life, then in a real sense that person is an embodiment of that essence. This person is respected and viewed from then on as an image of perfection that is identical with the essence, and there is a confusion between the historical person and the otherworldly archetype. This is how a saint, or divine human being, is recognized. Human limitations are transcended, and the historical person enters the realm of timelessness. Because the archetypes were seen as individual gods and goddesses, their qualities were conserved through the change from polytheism to monotheism.

ABOVE: Nuns were made subordinate to male priests as Christianity took over from paganism.

ABOVE RIGHT: The great St. Columba, an example of a person who transcended human limitations as a saint.

ST. BRIGID

ABOVE: The three aspects of the original goddess Brigid were transferred to St. Brigid.

The cultus of St. Brigid of Kildare encapsulates every aspect of Celtic religion. The original Brigid was a threefold goddess of light, fire, and healing, who was worshiped at the fire festival each year on February 2, called brigantia or imbolc. Bishop Cormac, in his ninth century *Glossary* describes Brigid as " A goddess whom the bards worshipped, for very great and noble was her perfection. Her sisters were Brigid, the woman of healing, and Brigid, the smith-woman." Thus when Christianity replaced polytheism, the attributes of the goddess were transferred to the saint of the same name. It is possible that

when the changeover came, a priestess-guardian of the shrine of Brigid became identified mythically with the goddess herself. Converted to Christianity, the former priestess was remembered by the church as the foundress of the Christian shrine of Kildare. It was natural that she should become the focus of devotion rather than the more abstract female deity. The qualities once ascribed to the goddess Brigit were transferred to St. Brigid, whose sacred place was maintained as a Christian shrine.

St. Brigid of Kildare is perhaps the most loved of all Irish saints. Her festival is Candlemas, celebrated on the old pagan festival day of Brigantia. Until 1220, a perpetual fire, tended by nineteen nuns, burned in a shrine near her church at Kildare. The fire was surrounded by a fence made of stakes and brushwood, inside which no man was allowed to enter. No bellows were used in keeping the fire burning, only the breath of women. This was none other than the fire of the old Celtic goddess, that was kept burning by the nuns, who maintained the best of the ancient Celtic traditions that they had inherited from the Druids. There were attempts to rekindle it in the 1990s.

St. Brigid is the epitome of kindness and charity. There are many stories of her assisting the poor, freeing slaves and interceding on behalf of unfortunate people. On one occasion, she paid a visit to her father, Dubtach, in Meath, and found him beating a woman servant. Immediately, she stopped the beating and reproved her father for his inhuman behavior. "Would to God you were always here to protect us from the master's violence," a servant told her. Because of this, St. Brigid is protectress of women. She was also kind to animals, calling wild geese and ducks to come to her so that she could caress them. Brigid was famous for the ale that she brewed, in prodigious quantities. It is said that, on one occasion, she supplied seventeen churches in Meath with ale from Maunday Thursday to Low Sunday. In addition to her patronage of brewing, she is patron saint of cooking and kitchens, and there is a prayer to bless kitchens that St. Brigid herself is believed to have composed:

"My kitchen,
The kitchen of the White God,
A kitchen which my King hath blessed,
A kitchen stocked with butter.
Mary's Son, my friend, come thou
To bless my kitchen.
The Prince of the World to the border,
May He bring abundance with Him."

☙☞

Under the name St. Ffraid, Brigid was a popular saint in Wales, and there are many churches called Llansantffraid in honor of her. In medieval times, before setting out, Welsh travelers would say the prayer, "St. Ffraid, bless us on our journey." Because she was a paragon of virtue, Brigid was sometimes confused with Our Lady. St. Broccan, who called Brigid, "The one-mother of the Great King's son," wrote a hymn to Brigid which begins,

"Brigid, mother of my King,
Of the Kingdom of Heaven,
best was she born."

☙☞

The Celtic church recognized more than one St. Brigid, though the original from Kildare is respected above all the others. All of these St. Brigids are, in their own ways, aspects of the archetypal goddess Brigid. Many of these St. Brigids, were the disciples of the original St. Brigid of Kildare. It is likely that they, too, were converted former devotees of the goddess. In Ireland at Candlemas, it is the custom for people to make special St. Brigid crosses out of rushes. The rushes must be pulled up, not cut, on St. Brigid's Eve, and must be woven from left to right. Then the Brigid's Cross is set up above the door, as a sacred protection for the house, and left there until the next year, when it is replaced with a new one. Traditionally, Brigid is welcomed back at her festival by rekindling the hearth fire after the house has been spring-cleaned.

ST. BEUNO

t. Beuno was a sixth century saint, the son of elderly, but noble, parents, whose birth was seen as something of a miracle. When he was old enough to be educated, he went to Caerwent, where he was taught by Tangusius. There he "obtained a knowledge of all the holy scriptures; afterwards, he learned the service of the Church and its rules, and took orders, and became a priest." Like many Celtic missionary saints, he traveled around, teaching and preaching, performing miracles and founding monasteries where his pupils could continue his work. His most important monastery was at Clynnog Fawr on the Lleyn Peninsula in northwest Wales.

He died there, after seeing a vision of angels descending from and ascending back to heaven. Beholding this wondrous sight, Beuno said, "I see the Trinity, and Peter and Paul and David the innocent, and Daniel, all the saints, and the prophets, and the apostles and martyrs appear. And I see seven angels standing before the throne of the most high Father, and all the fathers of heaven, singing their songs, and saying, 'Blessed is he whom thou hast chosen, and taken, and who does for ever dwell with Thee.'" Despite his orthodox life and death, Beuno was not known especially for his piety, but for the cultus that was practiced at his shrine for many centuries afterward.

Cattle were a vital element in the ancient northern European economy, and as such had an honored place in society and culture.

The Northern Tradition creation myth ascribes the coming into being of the world by means of the primal cow, Audhumla, and there are many instances of cattle-cults in central and northern Europe. The cattle-cult was continued in Christian times at several places in the Celtic realms, and Beuno's cult-place at Clynnog Fawr is one of the most evocative. It is clearly an old pagan holy place: megaliths are plentiful around the church, in its foundations, and the adjoining chapel of St. Beuno. It is clear that before the shrine of St. Beuno was built, there existed the cultus of a pagan deity to which bulls were offered. John Ansters, writing in 1589, told how cattle were offered to St. Beuno, "As that people are of the opinion, that Beyno his cattell will prosper marvellous well."

The cult of St. Beuno continued until the middle of the nineteenth century, a remarkable survival of ancient tradition. Until about that time in Wales, horned cattle and sheep were also eaten at feasts in honor of St. Ffraid, the Welsh version of St. Brigid. In Brittany, cow tails were offered to St. Herbot at his church near Huelgoet. At his pardon, cattle were driven round the church, then led to his holy well to drink the water. Bottles of water were taken home by participants who needed to treat sick cattle. At Carnac, in Brittany, the cattle traditions of St. Cornely are observed to this day.

ST. AELHAIARN

 egend tells us that this monk, who lived in the seventh century, was a servant of St. Beuno. Beuno used to walk into the middle of a river to pray and, on one occasion, was followed by his servant, curious to find out what he was up to. Beuno, not recognizing his servant, prayed that the man should be shown a lesson by God, and immediately he was set upon by a pack of wild animals, that tore him apart. Then, St. Beuno discovered that the man had been his disciple. So he collected up the bones and flesh, and set about reassembling the body. He put everything together, except for one part that was missing, an eyebrow. He used the iron tip of his pastoral staff to make a new eyebrow, and brought the dismembered man back to life. After that, he was called Aelhaiarn, "the iron eyebrow." Beuno's disciple followed in his footsteps and became a priest, tending a holy well near his church at Llanaelhaiarn, where sick people came to bathe and take the waters in the hope of the bodily restoration of which St. Aelhaiarn is a symbol, and the resurrection that Christians expect after death.

ST. MAELRUBHA

Not much is known about St. Maelrubha or Maree, other than that his name means "The Great King" and is thus an epithet rather than a personal name. Maelrubha is better known for his cultus than for his actions in life. It is clear that his cultus took over from an earlier pagan worship, localized in the Gaerloch region of Scotland, around Loch Maree and the holy island in it. In the seventeenth and eighteenth centuries, people were sacrificing bulls to Maelrubha to gain favors or to heal the sick. Even as late as the nineteenth century, people referred to him as "The God Maurie." His holy well on the island in Loch Maree was resorted to by insane people, who were ritually treated by resident men called derilans. Eventually, in the middle of the nineteenth century, the holy well dried up, and the rites ceased. But the mythos of Maelrubha still remains, a spiritual entity who is neither pagan god nor Christian saint.

ST. TEGLA

In former times, St. Tegla was one of the most invoked Celtic saints of healing and alleviation of suffering. Although little is known of her origins, her legend tells of her miraculous cures of seemingly impossible cases. For example, a man called Leffius, blind from birth, called upon St. Tegla. She appeared to him with two bright stars in her hand, that she placed in his eyeless sockets. Immediately, they were transformed into new eyes, and the blind man could see. A lord called Kinan called upon her to free him of the agonizing pains in his head. This she did, on condition that he free some prisoners that he was tormenting. Her shrines at Llandegla in Denbighshire and Llandegley in Radnorshire, were resorted to by people seeking cures, especially for epilepsy.

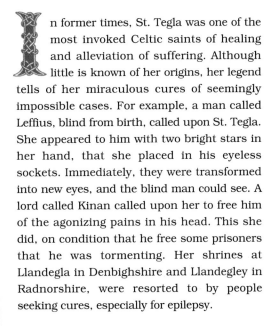

LEFT: The importance of cows to the economy brought about the veneration of cattle and cattle-cults. According to the legend of the Nothern Tradition, Audhumla, the primal cow, is responsible for the creation of the world.

The Hereditary Tradition

Chieftains and Priests

In traditional Celtic society, the family or clan had two hereditary leaders. One was the warlord or king, who commanded the clan in peace and war. The other, no less important, was the priest or Druid, who was the chief of the religious side of the clan. The members of the religious side were bound to the secular in that they had to perform religious ceremonies, while the secular side supported the religious with tithes and concessions. When the Christian religion was introduced, priests and monks occupied the social position that the sacred side had held previously. In pagan times, Druids were not allowed to carry weapons, and this concession was applied later to Christian monks and priests who had taken over the functions previously carried out by the Druids.

The pagan priestly function was hereditary, and it remained so once Christianity arrived. The scions, or descendants, of pagan priestly families became Christian priests, and took over the traditions and holy places from their pagan forebears. Their holy places were ancestral property, and passed to their newly Christian owners. The places were then reconsecrated, and monasteries or churches were built there in place of the sacred trees or standing stones. Their owners were remembered as the saints who had founded the churches. All over the Celtic realms, newly converted Christian monks and priests took the same career path as their ancestors had done before them in the old religion. In Ireland, Christian priests continued all of the Druidic functions, but reinterpreted their elements according to the new Christian beliefs and practices. When St. Patrick and St. Carantoc served as members of the Irish high king's legal commission, they assumed the law-giving role formerly taken by the Druids. Although they introduced some new Christian elements into Irish law, St. Patrick and the other members of the committee left much of the traditional structure in place.

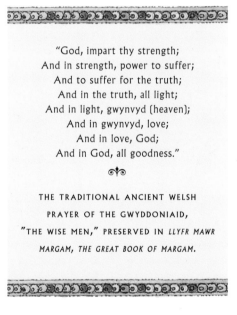

"God, impart thy strength;
And in strength, power to suffer;
And to suffer for the truth;
And in the truth, all light;
And in light, gwynvyd (heaven);
And in gwynvyd, love;
And in love, God;
And in God, all goodness."

THE TRADITIONAL ANCIENT WELSH
PRAYER OF THE GWYDDONIAID,
"THE WISE MEN," PRESERVED IN *LLYFR MAWR MARGAM, THE GREAT BOOK OF MARGAM.*

LEFT: Church and State had a close and equal relationship.

Saintly Genealogies

In the traditional genealogies, the British saints are accounted as belonging to one or other of the ancient noble families of Britain. These complex genealogies begin in the late Roman period and have been preserved in early medieval Welsh bardic manuscripts. According to their triadic view of things, the Welsh bards count three saintly tribes of Britain, those of Cunedda Wledig, St. Brychan, and Caw. The noble families include the race of Eudaf, descended from the lord whose daughter was St. Elen Luyddog, patron saint of the roads of Britain. St. Elen Luyddog married the usurping Roman emperor, Magnus Maximus, whose megalomania was responsible for the weakening of Britain's defences. He is counted as the founder of another of the noble families, the line of Maxen Wledig. The race of Eudaf includes the important saint, Tudwal, and a number of lesser saints, including Gwerydd, Iestin, Cadfrawd, and Gwrmael. The most important scion of this line was King Arthur. The line of Maxen Wledig, from whom over twenty saints issue, includes St. Owain Finddu, St. Lleuddad, St. Baglan, and St. Collen. The third family of British saints is descended from Coel Godebog. Among his descendants were St. Gwenddoleu, St. Deiniol, St. Asaph, and the great, but tragic king, St. Pabo Post Prydain, "The Pillar of Britain."

ABOVE: Many of the saints were members of noble families.

Descended from Ceol Godebog is the line of Gorwst Ledlwm, that includes St. Kentigern, St. Cadell, and also Medrod, the Mordred who slew King Arthur. The family of Amlawdd Wledig, King Arthur's grandfather, produced St. Tyfrydog, St. Teyrnog, and St. Tudur.

The family of Emyr Llydaw sired St. Germanus the Armorican, one of the earliest Christians living in the Isle of Man. The three-breasted patroness of nursing mothers, Gwen Tierbron, and her sons, St. Gwethenoc, St. James, and St. Winwaloe are, along with St. Padarn and St. Derfel Gadarn, the most notable saints of this line. The race of Cunedda Wledig, a lord who fathered twelve children, produced many of the more important Celtic saints, including St. Teilo, St. Seiriol, St. David, St. Gwen, St. Cybi, and St. Ailbe. The family of Cystennin Gorneu, or Constantine the Tyrant, produced St. Gildas, St. Dyfrig, and many other less important saints. Similarly, the race of Cadell Deyrnllwg bore numerous saints, including Cadell's son, St. Cyngen and his great-grandson, St. Beuno. Later generations of this same family also produced local and secondary saints such as St. Ystyffan, St. Cadoc, St. Eigion, and St. Gwyddloyw. Finally, the family of Gwrtheyrn Gwrtheneu gave rise to St. Edeyrn, St. Elldeyrn, St. Eurdeyrn, and St. Faustus.

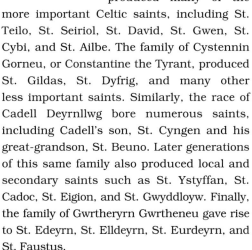

ST. NON

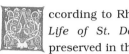ccording to Rhygyfarch's work, *The Life of St. David*, and traditions preserved in the former service book of her church at Altarnon, St. Non was the daughter of Anna, daughter of Gwrthefyr Fendigaid. On her father's side, she was also of noble birth, being the daughter of Cynyr of Caer Gawch. Like many Celtic saints, St. Non, who has the epithet Bendigaid, "Blessed," is also known by other names. In Britain, she appears as Nonna and Nonnita, and in Brittany as Melaria. St. Non is revered mainly because she was the mother of St. David, who eventually became the patron saint of Wales. Her most sacred place is at St. Non's Head in Pembrokeshire, west Wales. According to Rhygyfarch's account, one day a wandering monk, called Sant, was out hunting. Sant was no ordinary monk however, for he was the former king of Ceredigion and had abdicated to take up the religious life. By the River Teifi, Sant experienced some typical Celtic hunting omens. He chased a stag along the riverbank, and through the chase, discovered a colony of bees in a tree. He killed the stag, took the honey, and caught a fish in the river. The result of his hunt was that he had the produce of the beasts of the earth, water, and air. Having collected together his spoils, an angel, a being of fire, appeared to him, and told him that he must give a portion of his takings to the nearby monastery of Ty Gwyn at Maucan. These offerings, the angel said, represented the virtues of a son whom he would father.

Non was a student at the school of Ty Gwyn, one of the monasteries where women were permitted to study. There, Sant made Non pregnant. Shortly afterward, the traveling preacher, Gildas, came to the church of Ty Gwyn, and tried to conduct a service. But he was disempowered, and could not speak. The pregnant Non was hidden inside the church and, when Gildas called for any concealed persons to show themselves, she came out of her hiding place and left the church. Then Gildas discovered that his power of concentration was restored. The holy presence of the as yet unborn St. David had overwhelmed him. Non, pregnant with David, was threatened by "a certain man in the district, accounted a tyrant," so she left the monastic school and went to live in a cottage among the standing stones on the clifftop beyond Bryn y Garn.

ABOVE: Another of St. Non's holy places is her well at Dirinon, Brittany, France. Here the saint is depicted in a carving above the well.

Non gave birth to the baby at the standing stones during a thunderstorm. In addition to the thunder and lightning, other omens accompanied the birth of the baby, for the stone on which St. Non lay to give birth was split with the force of the birth, leaving the imprint of her hands upon it. One part of the stone remained behind St. Non's head and the other stood upright at her feet. This stone was later used as the altar slab in the chapel of St. Non. Another legend tells how, when the megalith was split, a spring welled up. This is the origin of the spring of St. Non, that is revered to this day for its curative powers. Writing of the holy well in 1811, the author Fenton noted, "The fame this consecrated spring had obtained is incredible, and still it is resorted to for many complaints. In my infancy... I was often dipped in it, and offerings, however trifling, even of a farthing or a pin, were made after each ablution, and the bottom of the well shone with votive brass. The spring... is of a most excellent quality, is reported to ebb and flow, and to be of wondrous efficacy in complaints of the eye."

According to legend, St. David was born dead, but St. Ailbe, who was present at the birth, resuscitated the baby, and baptized him in the spring. Then, the baby was taken away to be fostered by the bishop, and grew up to be one of the greatest Welsh churchmen. At the request of her sister, St. Gwen, St. Non later left Wales and went to Cornwall, where she founded the church of Altarnon. Like her original holy place in Pembrokeshire, the sacred enclosure of Altarnon was located at a holy well with healing properties. Like so many British saints, she also visited Brittany. She is remembered there by several church dedications and a mystery play of her life, Buhez Santes Nonn, that was performed for many years at her pardon at Dirinon.

ST. GWEN TEIRBRON

Another Celtic saint who absorbed the attributes of an earlier goddess is St. Gwen Teirbron, the patroness of nursing mothers. She was also an important saint in Brittany, though she was revered in Britain as St. White, St. Wita, or St. Candida. In former times, nursing mothers would offer St. Gwen Teirbron a distaff and some flax to ensure an adequate supply of breast milk for their babies. Her images depicted her with three breasts, symbolic of plenty. But in the 1870s, there was a drive by Breton priests to destroy or bury the images of Gwen as "somewhat outrageous and not conducive to devotion." Therefore few images of St. Gwen Teirbron still exist today, and she is less respected than in former times.

RIGHT: St. Anne, mother of the Virgin, is shown here tutoring her daughter. Celtic saints of similar names were revered as St. Anne after the conversion to Christianity.

THE MOTHER SAINT, ANNA

The story of the conception of the Breton saint, Hoernbiu, is almost identical to that of St. Non and St. David. According to the legend, an angel appeared in a dream to Hoernbiu's future father, Hoarvian. It told him that, although he had sworn a vow of celibacy, he was destined to encounter a woman called Rivanon. Traveling across country, Hoarvian came to a spring, and there was Rivanon, as predicted. This Christian reverence of St. Non and Rivanon, as mothers of saints, is, in some respects, a continuation of the ancient devotion to the ancestral goddess of the Celts. This mother of the gods, and ancestress of the Celtic nobility, was known under the names of Anna, Nonna, Dana, and other variants with the "nan" and "non" name elements. Whatever she is called, she is a very widespread deity, appearing in the Roman pantheon as Annona, goddess of the harvest, and in the Northern Tradition as Nanna, mother of the slain god, Balder. Many of the holy wells in the Celtic realms are sacred to St. Anne and to her variants. It is probable that, before the Christian religion, these wells were sacred to the goddess saint.

After the conversion to Christianity, some ancient images of these Celtic goddesses were revered as St. Anne, the mother of Our Lady, and grandmother of Jesus. The cult of St. Anne remains important in Britanny to this day. Images that were discovered in the earth by chance, were believed to have appeared in the world by means of divine grace. An important instance

of this occurred in 1625 at Keranna, in the parish of Plunevet, in Morbihan, Brittany. While plowing a field, a farmer, Yves Nicolayic, unearthed a statue. It was very probably an image of Bona Dea, one of the Gallo-Roman tutelary, or guardian, earth goddesses. But the devout Christian farmer saw his find as a female saint. He therefore took it to the local Carmelite monks who, as devotees of the cult of the mother of Our Lady, immediately recognized the figure of a woman holding two babies as St. Anne. They decided to construct a chapel to house the image, and dedicated the building to St. Anne. Because of the miraculous manner in which the image had appeared from the earth, pilgrims flocked to the chapel. Although the image was destroyed in the French Revolution, a new basilica was later built on the site of the old chapel in 1870 and today Sainte-Anne d'Auray is the major shrine of Brittany and is visited by tens of thousands of pilgrims each year.

ABOVE: One of the many holy wells sacred to St. Anne is to be found in Morbihan in Brittany, France.

RIGHT: A statue of St. Anne at her shrine in Sainte-Anne d'Auray, Brittany, France.

RIGHT: The Anglo-Saxon monarch, Edward the Confessor, is an example of a king who was recognized as a saint.

The Royal Saints

There is a tradition in the British Isles that makes departed kings into saints, complete with their own shrines and prayers. Among the royal saints are the founding fathers of noble families whose members included famous Christian holy men and women, or kings who abdicated to become devout holy men in later life. Benefactors to the church, and Welsh kings who died in battle against pagan enemies, or who were assassinated, were also given sainthood. The Anglo-Saxons too, conferred sainthood on their kings in continuance of the Germanic tradition of divine kingship. St. Oswald, who died fighting the pagan Mercians, the East Anglian king St. Sigebert, St. Ethelbert, and St. Edmund, and the Anglo-Saxon monarchs Edward the Martyr and Edward the Confessor, are all recognized as saints. The Celtic tradition celebrates the hero, and a Christian king who defeated his enemies, especially if they were pagan, was a prime candidate for sainthood. St. Rhydderch Hael, a descendant of Magnus Maximus, was sainted because he was victorious in the Battle of Arderydd in the year 573. This was the decisive battle in the Cumbrian civil war that was fought between a

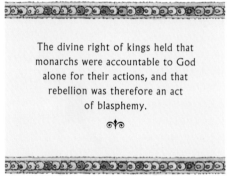

The divine right of kings held that monarchs were accountable to God alone for their actions, and that rebellion was therefore an act of blasphemy.

Christian faction composed of families of Roman descent, and a pagan one, composed of nationalist Britons. Having defeated his pagan rivals, Rhydderch Hael summoned St. Kentigern to Cumbria to extirpate the pagans. As a result he was considered the epitome of Christian kingship.

Kings who gave up their royal life to become monks are among the most interesting of the Celtic saints. The only way that a king could lose his title in those times was either to be assassinated or die in battle, or to renounce his power and become a monk. Also, in an era when it was a matter of honor to die with one's men if defeated in battle, becoming a monk was an alternative way of leaving the secular world. St. Pabo Post Prydain, "Pabo, the Pillar of the Britons," is an example of this. Pabo was a king in the north of Britain, who fought a rearguard action against Pictish invaders who overran his kingdom. When his warriors were defeated and his land was conquered, he fled to Wales where, having given up his royal title, he became a devout monk, and died in the year 595. He is counted as the oldest of the saints of Anglesey, where his foundation, Llanbabo, still exists.

ST. GWYNLLYW

The ex-king known as St. Gwynllyw, or St. Wooloo, is an example of how a bad king could repent and end his life considered a holy person. Gwynllyw Filwr, "The Warrior," seems to have started out as a robber baron who, through guile and bravery, elevated himself to the position of king of seven districts of Glamorgan, in south Wales. *The Life of St. Cadoc* tells us how this king "was given up to carnal allurements, and frequently instigated his guards to robbery and plunder, and lived altogether contrary to what is right, and disgraced his life with crimes." But, after many years of tyranny, Gwynllyw saw a vision of an angel, who showed him the enormity of his sins and urged him to become a man of peace and religion. His son, Cadoc, had, by now, become a Christian and risen to be respected as a saint. Through his mother, Gwladys, St. Cadoc was able to convince Gwynllyw that he should embrace Christianity, abdicate and become a monk. So he gave up his life of rapine, and sought an omen for his new monkish settlement. When he came across a white ox on a hill, he saw this as the omen, and built his cell there. After his death, it became the church of St. Wooloo, for Gwynllyw's reformed life was exemplary, and he was counted among the Celtic saints.

ST. CONSTANTINE

In the sixth century, St. Constantine was king of Dumnonia (now Somerset, Dorset, Devon and Cornwall, the West Country of England). He profaned the sanctuary of a church by entering it in the disguise of an abbot to kill the two sons of Mordred, King Arthur's killer. After living a life of infamy himself, Constantine underwent conversion to Christianity, and retired as a monk to Menevia (St. David's), where he lived out the remainder of his life in piety.

ST. CADWALADR FENDIGAID

Another sainted king was St. Cadwaladr Fendigaid, who was the last king to hold the title of Gwledig, "High King of Britain." As king of the Britons, his father, Cadwallon had fought on the side of the Anglian king of Mercia, Penda, who was a staunch pagan, against the Roman Catholic Northumbrians. Allied with the Mercians under King Penda, Cadwallon's forces were victorious at the Battle of Heathfield in 633, and the Northumbrian king, Edwin was slain. According to Bede, Cadwallon's war was an ethnic crusade, for he attempted to "cut off all the race of the English within the borders of Britain... Nor did he pay any respect to the Christian religion which had newly taken root among them; it being to this day the custom of the Britons not to pay any regard to the faith and religion of the English." When Cadwallon was killed in battle, "the last hero of the British race," the Britons were expelled from Northumbria, and Cadwallon was succeeded by his son, Cadwaladr.

Unlike his heroic father, Cadwallon, whose many honors included victory in fourteen battles and sixty skirmishes, King Cadwaladr was a Christian. He was not a warrior, and as a result his men considered him to be a coward who preferred to go to church rather than to lead his forces to victory over his enemies. Cadwaladr did not die in battle, but in bed of the plague, in the year 664. After his death, he was given the epithet Bendigaid, "Blessed," and was counted by the bards as one of the three blessed sovereigns of Britain, for the protection which he offered to Christian refugees. Paradoxically, after his death, like many dead leaders, the unwarlike St. Cadwaladr Fendigaid was believed to be waiting in the otherworld for the moment when he could return to lead the Britons to victory over their enemies. It was thought that this would happen at a great decisive battle that would reverse their fortunes. Armes Prydein, the prophecy which circulated during the early tenth century, spoke of just such a victorious return. It led to the crushing defeat of the Celto-Scandinavian confederation by the English forces of King Athelstan at the Battle of Brunanburgh, which in turn brought an end to Celtic power in Britain forever.

ABOVE: King Cadwaladr was a Christian. The fish design on this tomb is a well-known symbol of Christianity.

MARTYR KINGS

Throughout history, leaders have run the risk of assassination. In early medieval times, murdered kings were sainted as martyrs, even when they died for profane, rather than religious, reasons. When miracles occurred at their death, or by their tombs, then all the better. Selyf, or Salomon, King of Brittany, who was killed by rebels while in a church, was counted a martyr, and sainted. King Tewdrig, who had abdicated and handed over the kingdom to his son, Meurig, became a monk at Tintern Abbey. Later, Tewdrig died in battle against Saxon invaders, and is considered a saint. Although he chose a burial place on the Island of Echni (Flat Holm) in the Severn estuary, he was in fact buried elsewhere because of an omen. After his body had lain all night at the site of his death, a wagon appeared, drawn by two stags. Tewdrig's body was put into the wagon, which carried him to the banks of the River Severn, where it stopped of its own accord. There, at Mathern, Tewdrig is buried.

ST. DOGED FRENIN

St. Doged Frenin, who is mentioned in the romance Culhwch and Olwen, was another royal martyr. He died at the hands of a rival king, Cilydd, who, in order to steal his wife and daughter, mounted a military expedition against him, killed Doged and took the women captive. Because he died in defence of his land and family, he was made a saint. Another sainted king who had his burial place divined by cattle was St. Clydog. He ruled over the kingdom of Ewyas, that straddles the current border of England and Wales in the Herefordshire region, and was assassinated by a love rival during a hunt. His body was put into a cart drawn by two oxen, that pulled it towards the River Monnow. When the yoke broke, this was the omen for the burial place of the murdered king, and the church of Clodock was built there in memory of a king of "straight justice, a lover of peace, and of pure chastity, and of straight and perfect life that was cruelly slain by a false traitor." At his death, there were many miracles, "and at his tomb, many more."

ST. COEL HÊN

Some Celtic saint kings are the Christian equivalent of ancestral deities. St. Coel Hên, or Coel Godebog, is considered to be the ancestor of saints. Perhaps the Old King Cole of the nursery rhyme, Coel Hên was king in Ayrshire, and the father of St. Ceneu, St. Elen, and St. Gwawl. St. Brychan is said to have fathered up to thirty-two sons and at least twenty-four daughters by his three wives, Eurbrawst, Proestri, and Rhybrawst. Giraldus Cambrensis wrote of this saint, "the British histories testified that he had four-and-twenty daughters, all of whom, dedicated from their youth to religious observances, happily ended their lives in sanctity." According to one of the triads, he gave his many children and grandchildren "a liberal education, so that they might be able to show the Faith in Christ to the nation of the Welsh, whenever they were without the faith." In his *Polyolbion*, Michael Drayton referred to a legend that the twenty-four daughters of St. Brynach died virgins and were transformed into rivers, doubtless an identification of the Christian women with the old Celtic river goddesses:

"Who for their beauties rare and sanctitie of life,
To Rivers were transform'd; whose pureness
doth declare

How excellent they were, by being what they are:
Who dying virgins all, and Rivers now by Fate
To tell their former love to their unmarried state,
To Severne shape their course, which now their
forme doth bear."

☙❧

ST. CAW

Like St. Brychan, the king who was canonized as St. Caw was the sire of more than a score of sons, all of whom were considered heroes. The story of Culhwch and Owen in *The Mabinogion* lists twenty-one of Caw's children, many of whom went on to become Knights of the Round Table.

Benefactor Kings

A sainted king who was a benefactor of the church was St. Meurig ab Tewdrig ab Teithfall, King of Morganwg. Despite being excommunicated for breaking an oath and murdering his rival, Meurig was canonized after his death as a founder of churches. St. Einion is a better example of the benefactor king. He is considered saintly because, as well as being brother of St. Meirion and St. Seiriol, he founded the monastery at Penmon, on Anglesey, and gave the holy island of Bardsey to St. Cadfan. After his death, miracle cures were frequent at his tomb at Llanengan church in the Lleyn peninsula. The burial places of worthy kings were considered of great spiritual power in their own right. St. Gwrthefyr, otherwise known as King Vortimer, who fought the early Saxon settlers under Hengist and Horsa, was canonized for his patriotism. Although he insisted that his body should be buried at the place where the Saxons first entered Britain, as a talisman against further invasion, they could not, or would not, do this and so, it was said, the Saxons took the land.

St. Gweirydd ab Brochfael, King of Glamorgan, who lived towards the end of the ninth century, reigned at a time of "ungenial seasons" and "calamatous wickedness." He is an example of how a king can a be good and pious example to all people through troublesome and difficult times. Sadly, few kings who were just good men are included among the Celtic saints. Lesser British kings who were sainted include St. Cawrdaf, St. Cynllo, St. Erbin; St. Geraint, a martyr who died in battle; St. Huail, prince and martyr; St. Lleuddun of Edinburgh, and St. Ynyr Gwent. Sant, the father of St. David, was not made a saint.

BELOW: Legend says that many of St. Caw's sons were Knights of the Round Table, and that all of them were heroes. Caw was a king who was later canonized.

ABOVE: According to the symbolic story of the Fall of Britail, *The Elucidation*, the only way to restore peace to the country, was to find the Holy Grail.

The Fall of Britain

Between the years 43 and 410, Britain was effectively a colony of the Roman Empire. Of course, such a long period of time could never have been an uneventful period of unbroken peace and prosperity. There were periodic times of social unrest and economic decline and occasional attacks by the tribes of the unconquered north and the marauding barbarian seamen along the coasts. However, the occasional catastrophes were dealt with, and the province remained within the empire. But at the end of the fourth century and the beginning of the fifth, there was a succession of important events which brought about the decline of Romano-British civilization. The beginning of the fall of Britain is told in old Welsh tale, *The Dream of Maxen Wledig*, a complex story which is an allegory of the history of the Roman general, Clemens Maximus, whose personal ambition was a contributory factor to the downfall of Roman Britain, and its invasion by Germanic peoples from mainland Europe. Clemens Maximus, who had been born in Spain, was chief of staff of the Roman army in Britain. When the Roman province was threatened by the Picts and Scots, he organized a successful war against them. Hailed as a hero, he then used his popularity to gain personal control of Britain. Proclaimed as emperor by his legions in the year 383, Maximus assumed the title Magnus, "The Great," and set about challenging for the mastery of the western empire.

Magnus Maximus called up his auxiliary troops from the British population, assembled a large expeditionary force, and ferried it across the channel to challenge the forces of the emperor, Gratian, stationed in Paris. Outnumbered, Gratian and his forces retreated to the south, but at Lyon, the emperor was betrayed by the governor, and assassinated. Maximus, now in power in Gaul, negotiated for an accommodation with Theodosius, emperor of the east. Magnus Maximus thereby assumed control of the Gallic part of the empire, and set himself up as emperor at Trier. Soon, this success did not satisfy his ambitions, and he mounted an invasion of Italy, with the intention of taking Rome. But this was ill-advised, and Magnus was slain at Aquileia in the year 388.

This personal defeat however was less significant than the effect of his withdrawal of most of the fighting forces of Britain. The furtherance of his personal ambition had catastrophic results, leaving Britain almost defenceless against invading forces. Gildas reported that, "Britain is robbed of all her armed soldiery, her military supplies, her rulers, cruel though they were, and of her vigorous youth, who followed the footsteps of the aforementioned tyrant, and never returned." Paradoxically, although his selfish acts led to the collapse of Britain, some see him today as "The Father of Wales," from whom certain Welsh noble and saintly families were descended. Maximus's wife, Elen Luyddog, daughter of Eudaf, gave him seven children, five of whom are recognized as Celtic saints: St. Ednyfed, St. Cystennin, St. Gwythyr, St. Owain Finddu, and St. Peblig. Their other sons, Antonius and Dimet, are not considered saintly. Twenty-one Celtic saints are descended from this Roman tyrant and his Celtic wife, Helen, who is also reckoned a saint.

The Age of Warring Factions

After the unsaintly Maximus was slain, the western Empire was under the ineffective rule of a boy emperor, and Britain was attacked from all sides, by Irish, Pictish, and Germanic assailants. But the security of Britain was eventually restored under the command of the general, Stilicho, in 399. However, the situation on the Continent was so bad, with the inroads of the Goths, that a significant part of the Roman forces were withdrawn in 401. In imitation of Magnus Maximus, a succession of generals in Britain engineered military coups, and set themselves up as emperors. The last of these was a man who took the title of Constantine III. In the winter of 406, an enormous contingent of Alans, Swabians, and Vandals crossed the frozen River Rhine into Gaul, almost without resistance. Constantine III, fearing that the barbarian army intended to invade Britain by way of the Channel ports, took his forces across to Gaul to occupy them. Constantine III's strategy was successful, and

ABOVE: The quest for the Holy Grail represents the attempts to restore the wasteland of Britain.

soon his army was fighting in Spain. Effectively, in 407, what remained of the Roman legions were withdrawn from Britain, leaving only a small local defence force, the Comes Britanniarum, in place. In his *De Bello Vandalico* (*On The Vandal War*), Procopius tells us, "Constantine was defeated on the battlefield. But the Romans were never able to recover Britain, which from then onwards was ruled by warlords." In 410, the *Gallic Chronicle* records that Britain was devastated by a Saxon attack. The fall of Britain was under way.

The Wasting of the Land of Logres

The medieval symbolic story, *The Elucidation*, describes the fall of Britain in symbolic terms. It tells how in former times, throughout the Land of Logres (Lloegria, the Welsh name for England), there were places called puis. These were holy springs of water whose existence empowered and fertilized the land. Wayfarers coming to any of the puis would be met by a fair damsel, who would offer them food and a golden chalice of refreshing drink. This symbolized the freely-giving abundance of the land, available for all. But then, a king called Amangons took one of the maidens captive, stole her chalice, and forced her to serve him alone. His men, seeing this, robbed and raped the other guardianesses of the wells. The survivors of these atrocities fled into the wild woods for safety, and the puis were abandoned. In the absence of the life-giving waters, the land became waste. Fields and flocks became barren, the bonds of society disintegrated, and law and order collapsed. The land was plunged into famine, pestilence, and social disorder.

In his travels through the wasteland of Logres, a knight called Blihis Blihiris encountered some of the former guardianesses and their children, living in impoverished conditions in the forest. They told him what had happened, and how the land had been destroyed by greed. The only way that the wasteland could be restored, they continued, was to find the Holy Grail, which alone had the power to bring back the former state of peace and plenty. The knight went to the court of King Arthur, and told him the whole story. Arthur summoned his knights, and the quest for the grail, the key to the restoration of the land, had begun.

Symbolically, *The Elucidation* reflects a real historical event, when both British society and the land did disintegrate from order into chaos. Having lost imperial support, the Roman institutions rapidly broke down. Without an administration, Roman imperial subsidies, or the means to collect local taxes, Britain suffered a financial and economic collapse. The infrastructure of towns and cities, roads, bridges, canals, aqueducts, sea walls, and military defences could no longer be maintained. So ex-Roman Britain, no longer defended by an effective navy and army, was invaded from the east by Anglians, Saxons, Jutes, and members of other Germanic nations. From the west came Irish raiders and settlers, and from the north, Pictish warriors crossed Hadrian's Wall, that had once defended Roman Britain. Small armies retained by local warlords were the only defense against the constant attacks.

Britain Alone

In the year 446, Gildas recalls, the British authorities sent a desperate letter to the Consul Aetius, pleading for Roman assistance against their barbarian invaders. "But in return, they received no assistance." Then, in desperation, the British king, Vortigern, who was a Pelagian Christian, sent for heathen Saxon mercenaries to assist him in the defence of his kingdom. Although it was not recognized at the time, this was the beginning of the settlement of the Germanic tribes who eventually became the English. The Saxon mercenaries eventually turned against their British paymasters, and began to the process of conquering Britain for themselves.

In his work, *The Ruin of Britain*, dating from about the year 540, Gildas tells how he was born in the year 497, the same year that Emrys Wledig, in Latin Ambrosius Aurelianus, overcame the Saxons at the Battle of Mount Badon. Before Emrys Wledig put up resistance to the invaders, the British were totally incapable of defending themselves against their attackers, and paid a high price for their incompetence in battle:

> "... all the chief cities were razed... all the inhabitants, prelates, priests and people were cut down, as the swords flashed around them, and the fires burned... there was no burial, except in in the ruined buildings... the wretched survivors were trapped in the mountains and slaughtered... others, crushed by starvation, surrendered to the enemy. Those who were not killed at once, were enslaved... Some emigrated overseas... Others resisted on their own land, though in constant fear."

☙❧

KING ARTHUR

Although historically there are few records of his life, Arthur, and not Emrys Wledig, is remembered as the British commander who halted the westward advance of Anglian and Saxon settlers. Perhaps his success came from a revival of the organization of the Comes Britanniarum, the old Roman local defence corps. However, unlike the other British kings who fought the Irish, Anglians, and Saxons, he alone is considered a paragon of Christian virtue. The Christian religion was the empowerment of the British warriors through religious rites that appear to have been an early form of the martial tradition that became chivalric knighthood in the later Middle Ages. At the Battle of Guinnion Fort, Nennius recounts, King Arthur "carried the image of the Holy Mary, the everlasting Virgin, on his shield, and the heathen were put to flight on that day, and there was a great massacre of them,

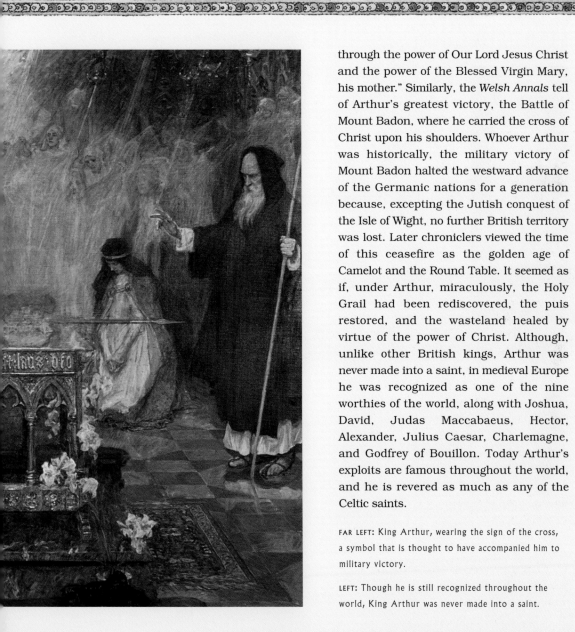

through the power of Our Lord Jesus Christ and the power of the Blessed Virgin Mary, his mother." Similarly, the *Welsh Annals* tell of Arthur's greatest victory, the Battle of Mount Badon, where he carried the cross of Christ upon his shoulders. Whoever Arthur was historically, the military victory of Mount Badon halted the westward advance of the Germanic nations for a generation because, excepting the Jutish conquest of the Isle of Wight, no further British territory was lost. Later chroniclers viewed the time of this ceasefire as the golden age of Camelot and the Round Table. It seemed as if, under Arthur, miraculously, the Holy Grail had been rediscovered, the puis restored, and the wasteland healed by virtue of the power of Christ. Although, unlike other British kings, Arthur was never made into a saint, in medieval Europe he was recognized as one of the nine worthies of the world, along with Joshua, David, Judas Maccabaeus, Hector, Alexander, Julius Caesar, Charlemagne, and Godfrey of Bouillon. Today Arthur's exploits are famous throughout the world, and he is revered as much as any of the Celtic saints.

FAR LEFT: King Arthur, wearing the sign of the cross, a symbol that is thought to have accompanied him to military victory.

LEFT: Though he is still recognized throughout the world, King Arthur was never made into a saint.

ST. ILLTYD

Unlike his knights, Launcelot and Gawain, who became monks, King Arthur was never to give up a life of warfare. But a recurring theme in Arthurian mythology concerns the knights who gave up their power and fortunes to take the ascetic life of the monk. A recurring theme in Christian mythology is the conversion of soldiers and knights away from their life of violence. St. Martin is the archetypal instance of the suddenly-converted warrior. Among the Celtic saints, the story of St. Illtyd is a classical example. St. Illtyd, now considered as one of the founders of the Welsh church, was the son of a British military nobleman, Bicanus, and his wife, Rieingulid. Rieingulid was the daughter of Anblaud, otherwise Amlawdd Wledig, king of Britain. Illtyd's aunt was

ABOVE: Launcelot gave up the life of warfare and became a monk. Here he is shown at the chapel.

RIGHT: The Celtic Monks produced beautiful artwork to decorate their gospels.

Igerna, King Arthur's mother, and his brother was St. Sadwrn. His education was in the hands of Germanus of Armorica, from whom he was to learn the seven sciences of classical learning.

Illtyd served as a knight with King Arthur, and then in the forces of the king of Glamorgan, Paul of Penychen. While out on a hunting expedition, Illtyd became separated from the group, who were destroyed when the earth opened up. Thankful that he had been spared destruction, he went to St. Cadoc, who told him that God had saved him. Illtyd thereupon gave up his military profession, left his wife, and became a monk in a cell by the River Hodnant. As with other ascetics, it is likely that Illtyd adapted his military exercises to religious purposes. We are told in a poem written between 1460 and 1520 by the bard, Lewys Morganwg, that:

> "The fasting and penance of his faith
> Would he, bare-headed, daily undergo;
> And each night, in a cold spring,
> Would he remain naked for a whole hour."

Another insight into the mind of the converted knight can be found in one of the bardic triads which is known as *The Sayings of the Wise*:

> "Hast thou heard the saying of Illtyd,
> The studious, golden-torced knight:
> 'Whoso doeth evil, evil betide him.'"

A common theme in these tales of kings and knights is the possibility of redeeming evil deeds by repentance and a change in lifestyle. As such they offer a role model for contemporary politicians and military men. As the writer of St. Samson's life tells us of St. Illtyd, "Of all the Britons, he was the most learned in all the scriptures... and in those of philosophy of every kind, specifically, of geometry and of rhetoric, grammar and arithmetic, and all of the theories of philosophy. And he was born a most wise magician, possessing knowledge of things to come."

After his conversion, Illtyd traveled around Brittany, Cornwall, and Wales, setting up monasteries and churches. His most important foundation was the monastery at Llantwit Major in south Wales. This became an important center of learning and, in later times, the burial place of a number of the kings of Glamorgan. Their commemorative crosses, which are some of the finest examples of Welsh Celtic art, can be seen today, at the church of Llantwit Major. Without practical experience of human life, and an all-round education, the Celtic monks could not have produced the masterful artwork we can see today in their gospels, ecclesiastical metalwork, and stone crosses. Thus, Celtic Christian learning did not extirpate the earlier traditions, but rather continued and developed them into a transcendent spiritual synthesis.

ST. HELEN LUYDDOG

St. Helen, wife of Magnus Maximus, is often confused with another saint, Helena, who was the mother of the emperor, Constantine the Great, who legalized Christianity in the Roman Empire. Although little is known about her historically, Helen Luyddog's name, "Elen of the Hosts," may allude to her prowess as a road maker, for many roads across Wales, called Sarn Helen, Ffordd Elen, and Llwybr Elen, bear her name. This may also be a garbled story of how the major roads of Britain, many of which are still in use today, were constructed by Roman engineers. There are also a number of holy wells in Wales named after her. She is not an insignificant saint, however, for she is the spiritual proctectress of travelers, and thus the Celtic counterpart of St. Christopher.

ST. BRYNACH

Although he was born in Ireland, St. Brynach is described in his Life as a "son of Israel," which seems to mean that he was of Jewish origin. His was a life of wandering, seeking somewhere to settle and worship God. As chaplain of the warlord, Brychan, Brynach came to Brecknock in Wales, which the Irish warrior had occupied during the troubled times. After making a pilgrimage to the Holy Land, where he killed a monster, St. Brynach returned to Wales, "floating over the sea on a stone." When he got back, the Welsh were in the process of expelling Irish settlers from Wales. Harassed as an Irishman, Brynach was attacked by would-be murderers, who wounded him seriously with a spear before he was rescued by friends. He was taken to a sacred source, the Redspring, where his friends washed his wound, and he was cured.

Escaping from the "ethnic cleansing," Brynach and his companions traveled from place to place until they set up a cell at a bridge at Abergwaun. Unfortunately, it was infested with evil spirits, and he was driven out. At the next place that they tried to settle, they were persecuted by the inhabitants, who stole the trees they had felled to make a building. At their next stop, they lit a fire, and were summoned by the lord who owned the land. The lord had not given Brynach permission to stop, but he greeted him warmly. The wandering was over. Brynach was given land at Nevern, close to the holy mountain of the angels, Carn Ingli, upon which he would go to commune with the inhabitants of heaven. Today, his church stands in a venerable grove of yew trees that bear witness to the ancient sanctity of Brynach's settlement.

ABOVE: Iona, where St. Kentigern visited St. Columba and exchanged pastoral staves with him.

ST. KENTIGERN

St. Kentigern, or Cynderyn, is one of the many Celtic saints who came from noble families. He lived in the sixth century, a contemporary of St. Columba. His mother, Thaneu, was the step-daughter of the king of the north British province of Leudonia. Unmarried, she became pregnant, and was sent to be stoned to death. But instead of carrying out their orders, her executioners put her in a cart and pushed it over a precipice on Mount Kepduf. She survived the attempt on her life, and a miraculous spring welled up in the ruts created by the cartwheels. When her executioners saw that she was still alive, they took her to the shore at Aberlessic, put her in an oarless coracle, and set her adrift on the sea. She survived again, and eventually came ashore close to the remains of a fire which some shepherds had made, and there she gave birth to Kentigern.

Just at this time, St. Serf passed by and, seeing the new-born baby, he adopted the mother and child, and gave the baby its name. Kentigern grew up at the saint's side, and was taught everything a priest ought to know. He was Serf's favorite pupil, being called Munghu, "dear pet," by his master. However, when he was older, Serf's other pupils turned against Kentigern, and he was forced to leave. He discovered the cell of a dying monk called Fergus, and carried out the monk's last wish that he be buried in a cemetery which St. Ninian had consecrated at Glasgow. Then Kentigern took over his duties. At the age of twenty-five, Kentigern was appointed bishop by the king of Strathclyde. Having gained supreme authority in the region, he went on a fact-finding tour, and discovered that most of the people were still pagan in their beliefs. The peasantry of the region were descended from the ancient Britons. So, "fostered by their Bards, who recalled the old traditions of the race before they had been Christianized under the Roman dominion," they restored their ancestral beliefs and customs. According to the *Red Book of St. Asaph*, around the year 550, forty years after the Roman legions withdrew, St. Kentigern discovered that "Paganism still lingered in the mountain parts near Carlisle," and made unsuccessful attempts to extirpate it. But instead of spreading Christianity, Kentigern's crusade stoked an ethno-religious political polarization in Cumbria. When political troubles flared up, Kentigern left Strathclyde and traveled south, to Wales, where he was summoned to St. David's. One day, seeing a wild boar digging in the earth near the River Elwy, he decided to build a monastery there. This he did, and soon Llanelwy had attracted 965 monks.

RIGHT: St. Kentigern, Glasgow's Patron is known, in the city, to this day, as St. Mungo.

But Kentigern was not to remain in west Wales, for eventually civil war broke out in Strathclyde. On one side was the traditionalist, pagan, "British party," led by Gwendoleu and Morcant, who claimed descent from the ancient Celtic noble family of Coel Hên. Opposing them was a Christian, "Roman party," under Rhydderch Hael. The Roman Christians claimed descent from Roman colonists and the regiments that had guarded Hadrian's Wall. In the year 573, the two opposing forces fought at Arderydd, on the west side of the River Esk, eight miles north of Carlisle. There, the supporters of Gwenddoleu and Morcant were defeated by the Christian army of Urien and Rhydderch Hael. After the victory, Rhydderch Hael declared himself king of Strathclyde, and summoned Kentigern to conduct a crusade to exterminate the pagans in his country.

After appointing St. Asaph as abbot of his monastery, Kentigern set out for the north with 665 monks and clerics. Back in Strathclyde's capital, Glasgow, Kentigern organized the extirpation of paganism. He forbade the popular practice of tattooing the body in honor of the gods, destroyed pagan shrines, and erected churches upon their ruins. Having Christianized the region, he sent his missionaries northward into the lands of the Picts, and further onward into the Orkneys and Norway. Kentigern visited St. Columba in Iona, and exchanged pastoral staves with him. Kentigern's staff, called Cathbhuaidh, "battle-victory," embellished with precious metals and stones, was kept in Ripon Cathedral until the fifteenth century.

To this day, the coat of arms of the city of Glasgow bears emblems that allude to a miraculous incident that took place there.

Rhydderch Hael's queen, Langueth, had a lover to whom she gave a ring that her husband had given her as a present. Seeing it on the man's finger as he slept, Rhydderch Hael pulled it off, and flung it into the River Clyde. Later, he ordered his wife to give him the ring back, on pain of death. Of course, her lover had lost it, and she could not. But when she told Kentigern, he prayed and was told that it was in the belly of a salmon in the river. A salmon was caught, and brought to the queen. When she cut it open, there was the ring, and as a result she was saved. The saint lived to a ripe old age, and was buried in the holy cemetery of St. Ninian, where Glasgow cathedral now stands.

ST. ASAPH

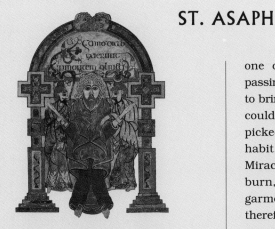

ABOVE: A page from the *Book of Kells,* the eighth-century illuminated manuscript of the Gospels.

St. Asaph was the grandson of the exiled and sainted king of northern Britain, Pabo Post Prydain. As a boy, he was schooled at the College of Elwy by St. Kentigern when he was in exile, avoiding the civil strife in Strathclyde. Asaph soon became recognized as the most able student at Llanelwy, which guaranteed him a bright future in the growing Celtic church. *The Life of St. Kentigern* tells us that Asaph was "distinguished by birth and presence, shining in virtues and miracles from the flower of his earliest youth. He sought to follow the life and teaching of his master." His exceptional powers were demonstrated once, when he was young, by a remarkable miracle. Asaph's mentor, Kentigern, would stand naked in cold water to say his prayers, even in wintertime. On one occasion, he was on the verge of passing out with the cold, and asked Asaph to bring him some burning coals so that he could get warm again. Asaph immediately picked up the hot coals in his monkish habit, and carried them to the old saint. Miraculously, the fiery charcoal did not burn, or even scorch, young Asaph's garment. It was a sign. "St. Kentigern, therefore, who up to that day had held the venerable boy Asaph dear and beloved, from that day henceforward regarded him as the dearest and best loved of all, and as soon as he conveniently could, raised him to holy orders."

Thus, Asaph became a priest. When the Christian party won supremacy in Strathclyde, the victorious king, Rhydderch Hael, invited Kentigern back to Glasgow. Kentigern appointed Asaph his successor, and he became head of the monastery. However, of the 965 monks at Llanelwy, 665 chose to depart with Kentigern, leaving only 300 under Asaph. According to *The Red Book of St. Asaph*, the saint was noted for "the sweetness of his conversation, the symmetry, vigour and elegance of his body, the virtues and sanctity of his heart, and the manifestation of his miracles." After his death, the monastery, which was also the seat of a bishop, became known as St. Asaph, and so it remains today.

C H A P T E R   V

Inroads and Conversions

The Saxons Advance

In the year 577, the west Saxons defeated British forces under the kings Ithail and Telpald at the Battle of Deorham, burned Gloucester and Bath, and occupied the land up to the River Severn and Bristol Channel. This was a significant victory, for in their advance westward, the Saxons had now succeeded in cutting the British held territories in two. No longer was what are now the areas of Wales, Lancashire, and Cumbria continuous with Dumnonia (Dorset, Devon, and Cornwall). Further inroads into British territory were sporadic, but the westward pressure continued, until in the year 607, an Anglian army commanded by Aethelfrith attempted to break through British territory to the Irish Sea. To prevent this, forces from four British kingdoms assembled south of the Mersey estuary. The forces of the British commander, Brochwel, king of Powys, were reinforced by those of Bledrws, prince of Cornwall, Meredydd, king of Dyfed, and Cadfan ab Iago, king of Gwynedd. The British army was assembled near Bangor Iscoed to fight the invader. In the ancient Celtic tradition, the monks of Dunawd monastery nearby, ascended a hill above the battlefield to curse the Anglians and pray for victory.

But the monks did not succeed in frightening the hardened Anglian fighting men. "Whether or not they bear arms," said the Anglian commander, "They fight against us when they cry against us to their God." So he ordered a detachment to ascend the hill to massacre the monks, who according to one account, numbered 200, and to another, 1,200. Fifty fled, including the British commander, Brochwel. The Anglo-Saxon victory at the Battle of Chester meant that the northern Britons were now cut off from the Welsh. Britain, as a unified country, had ceased to exist, and there were only three regions, separated by Anglo-Saxon held territory. In later years, the Anglo-Saxons were to conquer Dumnonia and Cumbria, leaving Wales as the only part of Great Britain still ruled by the descendants of the ancient Britons.

Factionalism Continues

After the consolidation of the invasion of Britain by Angles, Saxons, and Jutes, and their conversion to Christianity, there was still animosity between the kingdoms and principalities that composed Great Britain. This conflict was essentially ethnic, but it was compounded by religious sectarianism between a Roman Catholic faction, largely Anglo-Saxon, and a Celtic one, largely Welsh (British). When, in the year 597, St. Augustine came to southern England as a missionary, he tried to bring the Celtic and Catholic factions together. They met beneath an oak tree on the

LEFT: Remains of the Celtic monastery, Tintagel Castle, Cornwall.

borders between the Hwicce and the West Saxons. But the divisions were too great, the churches remained separate, and the mutual suspicions continued as before. In the seventh century, the chronicler Aldhelm wrote of how the Welsh clergy refused to officiate when Englishmen were present. Catholics who went to Wales were compelled to suffer forty days' penance before they could associate with the Celtic clergy, such was the suspicion. There are remnants of this old Welsh–English animosity in a legend of St. Beuno at Clynnog Fawr, in west Wales. The sacred oak tree of St. Beuno that grew in the churchyard there had a branch that curved down to the earth. It was said that if an Englishman should pass beneath the branch, he would die immediately by the power of St. Beuno, but should a Welshman go under it, no harm would befall him.

On the other side, the animosity was no less fierce. In his *Ecclesiastical History of the English People*, the eighth century Northumbrian monk, Bede, stated that the Celtic priests were inferior to the Roman Catholic ones. His reasons were that they "never preached the faith to the Saxons or Angles who inhabited Britain with them," so, according to Bede, "God in his goodness... appointed much worthier heralds of the truth to bring his people to the faith." Bede saw the massacre of Welsh monks by Anglian warriors at the Battle of Chester in the year 607 as the fulfilment of a prophecy that had been made by St. Augustine. This hostility between the Celtic and Catholic churches was only resolved when the Celtic Christians were compelled to adopt Catholic practices. This finally lead to the extinction of all Celtic practices and ultimately, to the end of Celtic religious identity.

ST. FURSEY

The ethnic enmity between the Britons and Anglo-Saxons, whether or not they were Christian, was not shared by the Irish. So, while Welsh monks remained separate, Irish monks traveled to the Anglian and Saxon regions of Britain in order to preach and found monasteries. Thus it was that St. Fursey, a member of the royal house of Munster, after receiving a vision of heaven and hell, came to East Anglia to found a monastery there. Fursey traveled from the shores of Lough Corrib to the easternmost part of England where, in the ruined Roman fortress at Burgh Castle, he set up his foundation around the year 631.

ST. AIDAN

Four years after St. Fursey set up his monastery in East Anglia, St. Aidan came from Iona with twelve other monks to the Northumbrian holy isle of Lindisfarne, where he also set up a monastery. Aidan's monastery was an important foothold for the Christian religion in Northumbria. Supported by King, later Saint, Oswald, Aidan traveled through the land preaching. An incident that took place one Easter links the two saints. It was customary for beggars and tramps to stand at the gates of the King's Hall waiting for alms. Aidan was ready to bless the royal feast inside, when Oswald picked up a huge silver plate of food and took it to the gate. There, he distributed both food and pieces of the silver plate to the poor. Aidan then took the king's right hand and blessed it for his compassion. Later, after Oswald died in battle with the Mercians, his hand was preserved as a holy relic that could cure the sick. The king gave Aidan many things to help him in his missionary travels, but he never used them. He even gave away a horse that the king had given him to save his feet from the rocky roads.

Another story found in a gloss in the *Felire of Oengus* tells us an amusing tale of some British bishops who went from Wales to Ireland to visit St. Aidan, who was assisting in the reestablishment of Christianity there, after its decline following the death of St. Patrick. When the bishops arrived at the monastic hostel, they were tired and hungry. But it was Lent, a time of fasting, and so for their dinner, the steward brought them oat biscuits with leek soup. Thinking that this was rather inhospitable to men who had just arrived from a long, dangerous, and tiresome journey, the bishops insisted that they needed pork or beef. The steward went to Aidan and asked him if, despite it being Lent, it was permitted to give them meat. Immediately, Aidan ordered a bull to be slaughtered to provide the bishops with meat. Later, when they were about to leave, the bishops thanked Aidan for giving them meat. However, it was not a breach of the Lenten rules, because "The bullock you killed for us had been suckled on milk, and ate grass only, so that its flesh was actually milk and vegetables in condensed form. But we felt conscientious scruples about those biscuits, for they were full of weevils!"

ABOVE: St. Aidan traveled through the land preaching but would never accept help from others to ease his way.

Through the agency of various factions, the whole of Britain was being converted to the Christian religion, the first step towards its reunification. Today, Aidan's statue stands on Lindisfarne, looking heavenward. Behind him stands a Celtic cross.

ABOVE: St. Brynach's Cross in Nevern churchyard, Dyfed.

CHAPTER VI

The Celtic Church

Hermits and Monks

The origin of Christian monasteries was in the desert landscapes of Syria and Egypt, to which certain Christian priests retreated to live the contemplative life, far from civilization. The aim of these early monks was to recreate paradise on earth by reunifying the body and the spirit that, they believed, had become separated. Through techniques that brought the mind, body, and spirit into alignment with one

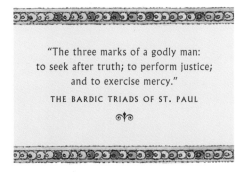

"The three marks of a godly man: to seek after truth; to perform justice; and to exercise mercy."

THE BARDIC TRIADS OF ST. PAUL

another, they strove to reestablish the human body as a point of contact between heaven and earth. St. Paul of Thebes (dec. 341) and St. Anthony of Egypt (dec. 356), the founders of this technique, believed that the fallen state of human beings was no more than an aberration from what is their natural state of grace. They taught that once disharmony was resolved, and spirit and matter had been brought back into alignment, humans could regain their true condition as the image of God in harmony with all creation. Once this had taken place, then the unnatural separation between the physical world and the spiritual world would finally be at an end, and the kingdom of God would be present on the material as well as the spiritual level.

Although the techniques used were often extremely ascetic, the potential reunion of human existence with the divine was not a rejection of the natural world. There was to be no war against nature, because nature is the manifestation of God's creative power. Early monks, like St. Anthony, lived without written matter, for they saw God's hand in the natural world. When a philosopher asked Anthony how he could do without the scriptures, he pointed to the landscape and answered, "My book, O philosopher, is the nature of created things, and it is present when I want to read the words of God."

Following St. Anthony's example, Celtic Christian intellectuals recognized that human beings are not external to nature. As early as the fourth century, a catechism ascribed to St. Ninian, teaches that the aim of Christian study is to "see in each herb and small animal, every bird and beast, and each man and woman, the eternal Word of God." In the tenth century Welsh in the *Juvencus Manuscript*, we are told, "The Father has made wonders in this world that it is difficult for us to find an equal number. Letters cannot contain it, letters cannot express it."

This vision of spirituality within nature is one of the most characteristic elements of Celtic religion. It is sad that in later times, so many Christians lost sight of this, and used certain Biblical texts as their excuse to rape and destroy the natural world.

Christians in Britain

Even before the collapse of Roman rule in southern Britain, Christian teachers and missionaries traveled to areas beyond the boundaries of the empire. At the time when the British theologian, Pelagius was teaching in Rome, in the year 397, St. Ninian, a British priest, traveled north into the land of the Picts to preach the Christian religion. There, in Galloway, at Whithorn, St. Ninian built a church. After the legions were withdrawn, but some time before Romanized Britain collapsed completely in the year 432, St. Patrick took Christianity to pagan Ireland. While Britain broke down through economic failure, disintegration of infrastructure, invasion, and civil strife, Ireland remained unaffected. The island had never been taken into the Roman Empire, and so there was no catastrophic change. St.

Patrick's mission was successful, and Irish society assimilated the Christian religion. A new church grew up in Ireland which, once it became established, began to spread across the sea.

Having been an important part of the former empire, the church in Britain retained strong connections with the Mediterranean region. Despite the invasions and wars, contacts had not been broken. Archaeologists have shown that, in the sixth century, more than a century after the withdrawal of the Roman legions, contemporary pottery from Alexandria, Athens, and Bordeaux was being used at Dinas Powys, the palace of the kings of Glywysing, in south Wales. Like all Roman religions, Celtic Christianity was cosmopolitan and syncretic. It adapted the liturgies and the theologies of Egyptian, Greek, and Frankish Christianity, incorporating them with elements of the older Celtic and classical paganism. Although many believers chose to live their lives in prayerful retreat, Celtic Christianity did not insist on isolation. Many Celtic saints undertook regular journeys and pilgrimages through mainland Europe, across the old Celtic heartlands, to the Mediterranean. In western and central Europe, Celtic saints founded many of the greatest monasteries, in which learning was maintained and from which it was disseminated.

Separate Identity

The asceticism of St. Paul and St. Anthony, which was adopted by the Celtic Christians, was called "white martyrdom," as opposed to the "red martyrdom" of those actively seeking to be killed in witness of belief. Throughout history, and in all cultures, humans have devised means of marking themselves out as members of special religious groups, and the Celtic monks were no exception. In addition to special clothing, or other physical signs, people have created bodily symbols of their religious allegiances. From circumcision as a sign of Judaism or Islam, to certain hair styles denoting Buddhist or Christian priesthood, these practices are still with us. There is some evidence that the pagan Celts were tattooed, and the Picts were especially associated with the practice and even named after it. Tattooing the body with emblems in honor of the gods was suppressed as heathenism in Britain in the time of St. Kentigern, returning later with the Crusades.

A shaven head, or tonsure, was the characteristic of a priest of the ancient Egyptian religion, so much so that St. Jerome advised that Christian priests should not appear with shorn heads lest they be mistaken for priests of Isis and Serapis. However, the Christian tonsure became the mark of a priest. The Egyptian tradition of shaving the whole head was adopted by the eastern church, being known as the Greek tonsure, or the tonsure of St. Paul. The Roman tonsure, otherwise called the tonsure of St. Peter, involved shaving the top of the head, leaving a ring of hair around it. In the Celtic realms, tonsures denoted certain ranks of society. Early Irish texts mention three kinds of tonsure: *airbacc giunnae*, the Druidic; *berrad manaig*, the ecclesiastical; and *berrad magad*, the slave's.

Being successors to the priests of the elder faith, Celtic Christian monks adopted a tonsure that was close to the Druidic one. This British and Irish tonsure involved shaving the front of the head from ear to ear. Because it was quite different from the tonsure of monks following the rule of St. Benedict, and was also the tonsure worn by Simon Magus, the pagan rival of St. Peter, it was seen by the Catholic monks as a sign of unorthodoxy.

The early desert monks were always remembered in Celtic tradition. In the British Isles there are a number of places dedicated to St. Anthony, such as Ffynnon Sant Antwn, a holy well of the saint, at Llanstephan on Cardigan Bay. St. Anthony is depicted on a number of surviving Celtic cross-slabs and high crosses, including those at Nash Manor, Glamorgan, in Wales and at Penmon on Anglesey. The thirteenth century *llyfr Du Caerfyrddin* (*The Black Book of Carmarthen*), speaks of "God whose name is One; God of Paul and Anthony."

ABOVE: Different styles of tonsure denote different ranks in society.

LEFT: St. Patrick was successful in his mission to bring Christianity to Ireland.

Deserts, East and West

There was trade between Alexandria and western Britain and Ireland in the late fifth century, when the ideas of the desert hermits and monks were current in Egypt. Around the year 470, a monastery was set up on the rocky Cornish headland of Tintagel. It is the earliest for which a date can be given, and it is in a place where trade with the East would have been made. The earliest Celtic monasteries were in caves, or consisted of collections of small stone cells or huts, rather like the retreats of the desert fathers of Syria and Egypt. These Celtic monasteries contained only a few monks, who lived independently of each other for most of the time, but got together to celebrate the sacraments. The church however, has always favored collective action, and later Celtic monasteries tended to be more coherent, centralized settlements.

In emulation of their eastern forebears, the early Celtic monks sought out "deserts," that is, uncultivated places far from human habitation or activity. The names of several Irish monasteries, like Dysert O'Dea, recall this tradition. Of course, the "deserts" of the north were nothing like the arid deserts of north Africa and Asia Minor. Cold and wet rather than hot and dry, these uninhabited regions teemed with wildlife, much of it dangerous to humans. This emphasizes the important difference between the Mediterranean tradition, where Christianity arose, and the Northern Tradition. In the hot Mediterranean region, arid deserts threaten to overwhelm and dry up civilization, while in northern Europe, the untamed wilderness threatens to invade and overgrow the fragile world of human beings. The danger of the northern "deserts" was thus quite different in character. Passive resistance is required to survive in the southern deserts, while active resistance is needed in the north. Rocky places, especially on islands or by the sea, were frequented by Celtic anchorites. In this way, wild places such as Scelig Mhichil and Iona became important monastic centers.

ABOVE: Merlin, or Myrddin, the enigmatic Celtic sage, counsellor, poet, visionary, and magician who counselled kings (Arthur and Vortigern). There are many stories about Merlin and his origins — some claim he was a king himself, some a god — and he has connections with both pagan and Christian traditions. At one period in his life, he was said to have gone mad and hidden away in the wild heart of Caleddon forest. This practice of self-exile to inhospitable places was also a feature of early Celtic monasticism.

ST. SEIRIOL

A saint who sought out "desert places" was St. Seiriol, one of the "Seven Cousins" who went on pilgrimage to Rome. On his return to Wales, he founded a monastery at the ancient Druidic holy place of Penmon, in Anglesey, that, in his time, had been abandoned.

In his *Caernaervonshire Antiquities*, Sir John Wynn of Gwydir (1553–1627) wrote, "Seiriol had also an hermitage at Penmaen Mawr, and there had a chapel where he did bestow much of his time in prayers, the place being then an uncouth desert and unfrequented rock and unaccessible both in regard of the steepness of the rock and also of the desertedness of the wilderness." St. Seiriol is remembered in the little holy island of Ynys Seiriol, otherwise known as Puffin Island, in the Irish Sea, to the north of Anglesey. However, like many Celtic hermits, St. Seiriol did not shun human contact, for he was a great friend of St. Cybi, who lived on the other side of Anglesey. They used to meet frequently at their holy wells at Clorach, in Llandyfrydog Parish, in the middle of the island. Seiriol, journeying from east to west in the morning, and from west to east in the afternoon, always had his back to the sun, while Cybi always walked with his face toward the sun. Thus, Seiriol was untanned, and known as Seiriol Wyn, "the Bright," while Cybi was Cybi Felyn, "the Dark." Symbolically, this tale tells us that, dark or light skinned, both were equally holy.

ST. TYDECHO

Another ascetic, Tydecho was St. Samson's brother. He epitomized the power of resistance against persecution. Tydecho lived in the district of Mawddwy, in central Wales, of which he was the spiritual guardian. He wore a horsehair shirt and slept on a blue rock without the comfort of a mattress. Local people tried to persecute him, but he always resisted them. On one occasion, the anti-Christian lord, Maelgwyn Gwynedd, turned the saint's horses loose in wintertime, hoping that they would die as a result. But, despite the snow and the cold, they returned, fatter and healthier than they had been before, having been protected by the saint's prayers and God's providence. Having failed to destroy the horses, Maelgwyn Gwynedd then stole Tydecho's oxen. But the saint harnessed deer to his plow instead, and continued his work, tilling the earth. Next, Maelgwyn brought his hounds to attack the deer, and sat on Tydecho's bed, the blue stone, in order to watch. When he tried to get up however, Maelgwyn found that he was stuck to the rock, and not was able to move. Finally, when he realized that he was fixed there by the power of the saint, he begged for Tydecho's forgiveness, and promised that he would never torment him again. Tydecho released him, and Maelgwyn gave back the oxen, and swore that his land should remain as a sanctuary "for a hundred ages."

ST. FINNIAN, ST. CIARAN, AND ST. KEVIN

The progress of Christianity in the British Isles was largely a matter of succession. A saint would found a monastery from which, perhaps twenty or thirty years later, would come missionary monks. They, in turn, would travel into unchristianized areas to settle and preach. All of the great Celtic monastic centers came into being in this way, and Celtic Christianity was carried to ethnically non-Celtic people. One of the early practitioners of this method was St. Finnian. Having been trained in Wales, he returned to his native Ireland and founded six monasteries. Clonard, in Meath, became the largest, eventually attracting 3,000 monks to live and pray there. In turn, in the year 545, one of the Clonard monks, St. Ciaran, established the monastery of Clonmacnois, which was later called Ireland's University. St. Kevin, who was at Ciaran's deathbed, lived in a pagan burial mound at Glendalough. But when, having attracted many followers, this place proved too small, he moved down the valley. There, St. Kevin set up the famous monastery of Glendalough.

ABOVE: St. Ciaran was originally a Clonard monk from the monastery of St. Finnian. He later founded a monastery himself and called it Clonmacnois.

RIGHT: St. Columba preaching on the island of Iona, where he established his monastery.

ST. COLUMBA

Born in County Donegal in the year 521, Saint Columba, arguably the most influential Celtic saint, founded monasteries at Derry, Durrow, and Kells. Often, he is called Columbkille to distinguish him from other saints called after the "dove of God," Columba. *Kille* means a monastic church, and he bears the epithet as the founder of the monastic rule that spread to northern England. When he was forty-one, he left Ireland and sailed to Iona, an island off the west coast of Scotland, a place from which Ireland cannot be seen. He had copied St. Finnian's prayer book without permission and, when he was forced to give the copy to its proper owner, St. Finnian was so enraged that a battle ensued, leading to Columba's exile. When he arrived on the old Druidic island, St. Columba expelled the resident women of Iona, so that he could set up an exclusively male monastery. The cows were deported too, because, as Columba said, "Where there is a cow, there is a woman, and where there is a woman, there is mischief." His was the monastery that Bede praised for the "purity of life, love of God, and strict adherence to the monastic rule." His monks followed the old Irish adage, relying on the bare necessities of life, "Mátá ocras ort ith, mátárt ort ól, mátácodladh ort luigh, mátátuirse ort suigh," meaning "If you are hungry, eat, if you are thirsty, drink, if you are sleepy, lie down, if you are tired, sit."

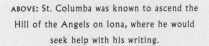

ABOVE: St. Columba was known to ascend the Hill of the Angels on Iona, where he would seek help with his writing.

However, in spite of his misogyny, there are many stories of how St. Columba alleviated the suffering of local people. His biographer, Abbot Adomnan of Iona, tells of how the saint consecrated a magic spear that provided a hungry family with food. Meeting a beggar on the shores of Lochaber one day, St. Columba ordered him to fetch a wooden stave from the nearby wood. Columba then sharpened it and blessed it so that "so long as thou hast this stake there will never be wanting in thy house an abundant supply of deer's flesh." Setting the stake in the ground, the saint and beggar departed. When the beggar returned the next morning, a stag was impaled upon the stake. And whenever the beggar needed food, a stag would run into the holy stake of St. Columba and kill itself.

To reduce the dangers to humans on his island, St. Columba extirpated the snakes of Iona, using his holy powers so that "the poison of no vipers shall have the power to harm either men or cattle within the borders of this island, so long as the inhabitants that dwell here shall observe the commands of Christ." Adomnan tells us that, on one occasion, when St. Columba was on the Isle of Skye, "entering a thick wood he met a boar of extraordinary size, which the hounds happened to be chasing. And seeing him from a distance, the saint stood still watching him. Then, invoking the name of God, and raising his holy hand, with earnest prayer he said to him 'Come no further in this direction; on the spot to which though hast now come, die!'" The boar, we are told, "fell down, killed by the very power of his word."

St. Columba also had an encounter with the beast now identified as the Loch Ness monster. Visiting the land of the Picts, Columba had to cross the River Nesa, where he saw some people burying a dead man. They told the saint that, shortly before he had arrived, a water monster had savaged the man while swimming. Columba ordered one of his companions to swim across the river to recover a small boat, called a coble, that was beached on the other shore. Once in the water, the swimmer attracted the beast, that surfaced, about to strike the swimmer. Immediately, Columba made the sign of the cross with his hand and, invoking God's name, commanded the monster, "Go thou no further, nor touch the man. Go back at once." Other texts tell how other Celtic saints also commanded water monsters. Colgan's *Acta Sanctorum* describes how both St. Colman of Dromore and St. Molua saved people from lake monsters.

On occasion, St. Columba would ascend the Hill of the Angels on Iona (called Sithean Mor or Cnoc Angel) to consult the angels. St. Columba is credited with writing around three hundred books, in addition to many poems and hymns. After his death, his books were held to have magical powers. His prayer book was used as a talisman to make rain in time of drought and as a protection for warriors who were about to go into battle.

Among Columba's writings was a series of prophecies. The Celtic saints were the heirs of two distinct traditions of prophecy. Firstly, there is the Celtic tradition of seership, which was the preserve of the *vates*, or prophets. Utterances such as the *Prophecies of Merlin* are among this type. The second is the ancient Jewish current of prophecy that culminated in the *Revelation of St. John the Divine*. Both prophetic currents have the tendency to foretell ruin, such as the decay of morals, the acts of tyrants, and the coming of wars, invasions, plagues, famines, and natural disasters. Columba's prophecies were collected together after his death by Abbot Adomnan. Some come from Columba's own writings, preserved in the *Book of Cummene the White*, while others were transmitted orally. The prophecies were addressed to St. Brendan and St. Boithin. They are preserved in an ancient Irish text containing many verses such as:

"Storms, plagues and biting famine shall prevail.
The seasons will forsake their regular course;
Plague will destroy the powerful
as well as the weak
With painful contortions of a
half-day's endurance.

Death will be the oppressor through all the land,
Despite abundance of food on one side
Thousands will die of starvation –
the houses shall be filled.
After wards the land
will become a barren waste."

As with all apocalyptic texts like *The Book of Revelation*, the end of the world is prophesied, following the tradition that St. Patrick had an agreement with God that no Irishman should be alive during the reign of the Antichrist before the Last Judgment:

"I give them a favour without deception,
As did St. Patrick the same;
That seven years before the Last Day,
The sea shall overwhelm Erin in one great flood."

In his last days, having been warned by God, through his horse, of his impending death, Columba wrote a prayer of hope, dictated to the monks tending him, "See that you are at peace among yourselves, my children, and love one another. Take the example of the good men of ancient times, and God will comfort and aid you, both in this world and in the world to come."

Celtic tradition asserts that highly developed spiritual people can produce spiritual flames, manifestations of the Holy Spirit. Abbot Adomnan tells how on Iona, the saint was sometimes seen enveloped in spiritual fire. On one occasion, "St Brendan saw a certain blazing and most luminous globe of fire burning over St. Columba's head and rising up like a pillar as he stood before the altar consecrating the holy oblation." At another time, as Virgno and Columba were praying at night, "a golden light descended from heaven and filled all that part of the church" where Columba stood. At his death, Adomnan tells us that Columba's church was filled with "angelic light."

It is a widely held Celtic belief that when the soul departs the body, it leaves in the form of a flame or light. When a person dies, his or her spirit is sometimes seen to leave the body in the form of supernatural light, that hovers above the house before dissipating. In his *Ecclesiastical History of the English People*, St. Bede tells how, after his death in battle at Maserfeld, a pillar of light stood over the remains of the Northumbrian king and saint, Oswald. This light column stretched from the wagon upon which the corpse lay, heavenward. Traditionally, such otherworldly lights at burial places are viewed as omens of impending death. It is believed, in Wales, that when a light appears at a certain spot, it foretells a death that is destined to occur there. But it does not necessarily mean that it is the witness who will die. This is not the case when phantom flames appear around buildings, for they signify a forthcoming death within. Occasionally, such lights are seen shining on old Celtic cemetery islands, such as Mun, in Loch Leven, Scotland.

LEFT: St. Columba with the old white horse that warned him of his impending death.

ST. TYSSILIO

Like their Irish parallels, some Welsh saints are best known as founders of monasteries and churches. St. Tyssilio, who was the grandson of the tragic king, Pabo Post Prydain, lived at the time of the Battle of Chester, when the Saxons broke through to split the land held in the west by the Britons. After this, Tyssilio fled from Wales, and lived for a time in Brittany. After his return to his native land, he busied himself in church founding. In the traditional manner of the Celts, the bard, Cynddelw recorded Tyssilio's churches in poetic form:

"A church raised with his fostering hand,
The church of Llugryn,
with a chancel for Mass;
The church beyond the shore —
beyond the glassy flood;
The church filled to overflowing,
beyond the palace of Dinorben;
The church of Llydaw,
through the influence of liberality;
The church of Pengwern, chiefest in the land;
The church of Powys, paradise most fair;
The church of Cammarch,
with a hand of respect for the owner."

Celtic Travelers

The Great Celtic Monasteries

In the late sixth and early seventh centuries, large monasteries, the size of small cities, came into existence in northern Europe. The monastery at Bangor-is-coed, in north Wales, Bede tells us, had "so large a number of monks, that when it was split up into seven divisions with superiors over each one, no part had less than three hundred men in it." The monastery of Bangor, on Belfast Lough in the north of Ireland, housed an even larger number of monks, reputed to be over 3,000 strong. As the largest center of Celtic Christianity, Bangor was able to send out many missionaries, who spread all across western and central Europe. In early times, Saxon and Anglian priests who were shunned by the Christian Britons, were trained by Celtic monks in Ireland. Often, English candidates for the priesthood would voyage to Ireland for instruction. Agilbercht, Saxon Bishop of Wessex in the seventh century, became a priest there. Along with their British counterparts, Irish monks were very active in Britain. Among the famous monasteries they founded were the abbeys of Glastonbury, Iona, Lindisfarne, and Malmesbury. Among the famous missionaries sent out from Bangor was St. Sinell, who went southward to set up monasteries at Luxeuil in France, and Bobbio, in the Apennines of Italy.

The Celtic Church in England

Because of the ethnic enmity between the Britons and the Anglo-Saxons, there were no attempts by British (Welsh) Celtic Christians to evangelize England. It was from Iona, the Scottish foundation, that monks came south into heathen England. The first of the Iona monks who traveled to the east coast of England was Corman. For some time, he tried to find a place to settle and preach in the Anglian kingdom of Northumbria, but returned having failed. Next, St. Aidan went to Holy Island situated off the Northumbrian coast and set up the monastery of Lindisfarne there. After sixteen years in Northumbria, Aidan died in the year 651. From Holy Island came St. Chad and St. Cedd. They went among the Anglians in Mercia and East Anglia. St. Chad set up the cathedral at Lichfield, where he meditated, spending all night up to his neck in a holy well. St. Cedd's church at Bradwell-on-Sea, in Essex, still exists.

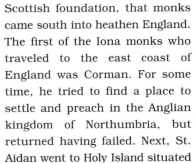

LEFT: St. David is credited with founding twelve monasteries, the most famous being that which bears his name.

ABOVE: Lindisfarne Priory, which was founded by St. Aidan on Holy Island off the Northumbrian coast.

Monastic Education

The earliest commentators on the Celts tell us that, among them, understanding and knowledge were the most prized abilities in any person. In Pagan times, the Druids and bards were highly educated men, who sought excellence in all things. Following their tradition, the monks and priests of the Celtic Church were also highly learned and respected men. So much so, that in the sixth century, Celtic monks continued to teach and preserve the classical literary tradition at a time when Roman civilization in the west was disintegrating. This was the time when, in what is now France, Gregory of Tours bewailed the fact that, "Culture and education are perishing, dying out in every city of Gaul... People often complain 'Alas for our times, literacy is dying among us, and no man can be found among our people who can write down the events of the present day.'"

However, the reverse was the case in Ireland, where the monastic schools were recognized as the best in western Europe. Writing later, Bede records how "In Ireland, there were many Englishmen, both noblemen and commoners, who journeyed from their motherland in the time of Bishops Finan and Colman... some soon took to themselves the monastic vow, but others deemed it preferable to travel between the cells of various teachers for the joy of reading. The Irish made all of them welcome, gave them food and lodging without charge, lent them their books and instructed them for free." The education at Celtic Christian schools was very wide ranging. Of course, their main teachings were religious, and based upon Biblical tradition, but this was not all, because they also included classical literature and the indigenous wisdom valued

ABOVE: Monks and priests of the Celtic church followed the tradition of the Druids and bards and were highly educated and learned.

by the former Druids. Thus, the leading Celtic saints were highly educated men, and respected wherever they went.

However, not every monastery was open to all and, in many places, women were shunned. Some Celtic monasteries were extremely exclusive. St. Malo would only allow ordained priests within the earthwork of his sanctuary. The Irish saint, Senan excluded women from his monastic island of Iniscathy, while today, the Greek Orthodox monastery at Mount Athos, in Greece, still has the rule that not only women, but all female animals, are prohibited from entering the holy place. The Celtic monastery at Sark, one of the Channel Islands, had the same misogynist rule, and it is only since the 1980s that the resident monks have allowed women visitors to set foot on Caldey Island in west Wales.

In some monasteries, only the inner enclosure, with its church and monks' refectory, was prohibited to women. In Brittany, for instance, no woman entered the inner enclosure of the monastery at Landevenec for over 400 years between the fifth and ninth centuries. Despite these examples, misogyny was not an overall policy, for there were notable exceptions like St. Ciaran.

ST. COLUMBANUS

 great missionary from Bangor, St. Sinell's pupil, Columbanus was born in 543. St. Columbanus founded even more sacred places than his mentor and was one of the most learned of all the Celtic saints. The medieval chronicler, John of Tritheim, called him "Prince of Druids," a title of great honor. In addition to being well versed in Christian theology, Columbanus was a lover of the works of the Roman poet, Ovid, and composed his own poetry in Greek. So, as well as theology and literature, in his monastic foundations, Columbanus' monks also taught astronomy, mathematics, geometry, and the handicrafts.

Among his most successful foundations is the Abbey of Luxeuil, in the old Celtic holy land of the Vosges. There, St. Columbanus founded his own monastic rule, that was considered harsh even in his day. Despite this, he and his disciples successfully set up about a hundred monasteries in mainland Europe. By the time the Celtic church was superseded, Celtic monks had founded monasteries in what are now France, Germany, Switzerland, Austria, and Italy. Their monasteries at St. Gall, St. Bertin, St. Riquier, Chelles, Echternach, Hanau, Jouarre, Jumièges, Lagny, Luxeuil, Noirmoutier, Remirement, and Wırzburg were important centers of the Christian religion throughout the Middle Ages, and many remain so today. Some of these grew to the size of large towns. For example, by the year 664, the monastery of Jumièges had 900 monks. These rich and populous monasteries, on important trade routes across the Continent, provided a network of hostels at which Celtic wayfarers could stay on their pilgrimages.

ST. CIARAN

The Irish saint, Ciaran, was much better disposed towards women than some of the other Celtic priests. Ciaran was willing to teach them and bring them into the monastic life. At his suggestion, Liadhain, his mother, founded a convent for women at Killeen, and his biographer tells us that "A maiden came to Ciaran, and he made her a Christian, and a true servant of God; and Ciaran constructed for her a little honorable cell near to the monastery, and he gathered other holy virgins around her." St. Non, the mother of St. David, was a pupil at the monastic school of Ty Gwyn, whilst St. Brigid is remembered for her great nunnery at Kildare.

According to legend, St. Ciaran's companions were a badger, a wild boar, a doe, a fox, and a wolf. We can take this literally, as an example of his living in harmony with the local wildlife, and also as representing his human followers through their totemic beasts, for his uncle, Laighniadh Faeladh, was known as "wolf-like," and his disciple, St. Sinnach, was of the clan Hy Sinnach, "the Foxes." Throughout Europe, traditional spirituality has always recognized the link between human beings and otherworldly powers. This has meant that in former times, people were always aware of the immediate presence of the divine, that could manifest at any time and in many different ways. So in Celtic spirituality, believers always recognize that at any time some unexpected manifestation may take place. The recorded lives of many early members of the Celtic church tell of the varied ways in which the voices of the otherworld communicate with them, spurring them to action on the material plane.

ST. DAVID

St. David is revered today as the patron saint of Wales. The story of his birth has already been told in the account of St. Non, his mother. He was born during a thunderstorm, an omen that he was to be a great man. When he was old enough, David was sent to the monastery of Yr Henllwyn (The Old Bush) for instruction in the Christian religion. As his biographer, Rhygyfarch, tells us, "David grew up full of grace and lovely to be looked at. And he learned the rudiments, the psalms, the lessons of the whole year, and the Mass and Communion; and there his fellow disciples saw a dove with a golden beak playing about his lips, teaching him, and singing the hymns of God." After more than ten years of learning, David set out to spread the word. According to Rhygyfarch, "he founded twelve monasteries to the praise of God. First going to Glastonbury, he erected a church there, and then he went to Bath, and there blessing the deadly water he rendered it salutary for the washing of

ABOVE: St. David, shown here with St. Winifred and the Virgin Mary, was a kind and caring saint.

bodies, and communicated to it perpetual heat." His most famous and lasting foundation was the monastery that bears his name, St. David's. After his death, his status grew, and eventually he was recognized as the patron saint of Wales, but only after the bones of St. Gwenfrewi were removed to England, as explained in Chapter 11.

While some saints were intolerant and violent, St. David is known only for the humane values that he taught and lived by. In his *Life of the Saint*, Rhigyfarch tells us that "He spent all day, never turning from his task nor wearying, in teaching and kneeling in prayer and caring for the brethren; also he fed innumerable orphans, waifs, widows, the poor, the sick, the weak and pilgrims. So he started, so he continued, so he ended." The means to living a humane life are alluded to in St. David's last address to his disciples that is recorded by several old Welsh chroniclers. In essence, it was, "Lords, brothers and sisters, be happy and keep the faith, and do those little things you have seen me do and heard me say." The "little things" that St. David emphasized are the everyday actions of mutual kindness and support without which society must disintegrate. He taught that harmonious relationships between humans can only come when we have respect for each other and for God. God's natural order is one of mutual support within the community. It is not maintained by everyone having a selfish disregard for others. It is a message of charity and kindness, the antidote to rootlessness, being "at home" with our neighbors and the divine. This is the teaching that contemporary Celtic Christians choose to follow, not that of the warrior monks.

Celtic spirituality teaches that all things in life must be done mindfully; there is nothing from which the spiritual dimension can be excluded. So there are prayers for all things in life. Some are in the form of words, while others are expressed by actions and deeds. Whether we are getting up in the morning, at work, walking through the country, sitting at a meal, or going to bed, we should always be aware of the divine presence. How this can be done is recorded in a piece entitled *The Mode of Taking Food and Drink*, from the ancient Welsh text, *The Rudiments of Divinity*:

"When thou takest thy food, think of Him who gives it, namely, God, and whilst thinking of His Name, with the word put the first morsel in thy mouth, thank God for it, and entreat His grace and blessing upon it, that it may be for the health of thy body and mind; then thy drink in the same manner. And upon any other thing or quantity, which thy canst not take with the Name of God in thy mind, entreat His grace and blessing, lest it should prove an injury and a curse to thee."

☙❧

ST. CUTHBERT

While working as a shepherd in southern Scotland, a young man named Cuthbert beheld a column of light descending from heaven to earth and, within it, a band of angels carrying the soul of a holy person to heaven. Inspired by this vision, he gave up sheep herding and enrolled as a monk at the nearby Melrose Abbey. When St. Aidan died, Cuthbert heard about Lindisfarne, and transferred himself there. After ten years, in 661, St. Cuthbert became abbot of that monastery, though he spent much of his time in solitary isolation on St. Cuthbert's Isle nearby. Like Chad and several other Celtic saints, Cuthbert meditated in water, standing waist-deep in the sea for long periods during the night. After such sea visits, sea otters would dry his legs. His connection with the natural world was also expressed in the story that when he and his monks were hungry, an osprey came to him with a salmon that it had just caught. Cuthbert cut the fish in half, half for him and his companions, and half for the bird.

ABOVE: St. Cuthbert saw a vision of angels as he guarded his sheep. The vision inspired him to take up monastic life.

After his death, Cuthbert's body was buried at the monastery on Holy Island. But it was exhumed by monks after the first Viking raid in the year 793, and carried around the country on a wagon. When, after years of traveling, they came to a place called Dunholm, they saw a dun cow sitting on the ground. This was the omen they had sought, and there they buried the coffin of St. Cuthbert. Around it, they erected a church that later became the great cathedral of Durham. We can still see a carving of the cow on the medieval cathedral, and the common public house sign, The Durham Ox, still commemorates the burial place of St. Cuthbert.

ST. BRENDAN OF CLONFERT

As well as traveling great distances overland through hostile territory, Irish priests were remarkable sailors. Their voyages are legendary, being retold in sagas such as the *Life of St. Brendan the Navigator*. With a few followers in a skin-covered frame boat, St. Brendan of Clonfert sailed in the hostile waters of the north Atlantic, visiting other-worldly islands with mythological characteristics. One island upon which they landed and lit a fire, began to move. It was a whale! In addition to being a forerunner of the intrepid European navigators of later times, Brendan was a benevolent founder of monasteries in Ireland and Brittany. A holy mountain in the west of Ireland, still resorted to by pilgrims, is Brandon Hill, the sacred peak of this saint.

Brendan's voyages, though embellished and mythologized by generations of story tellers, tell of real expeditions by sea made by brave Irish monks to the islands that lie in the northwest Atlantic. From Ireland, Celtic monks first sailed to the local islands, such as Scelig Mhichil and the Arans, where they set up religious settlements. Later, St. Columba

colonized Iona, to the west of Scotland, and his followers founded more monasteries in the Orkney and Shetland Islands. There, islands that bear the name "Papa" recall the priests who once lived and prayed there. Around the year 700, voyaging Irish monks discovered the Faeroe Islands, where their desecendants lived until around 860, when they were expelled by the Vikings. In the 790s, sailing even further north, into the Arctic, Celtic monks reached Iceland, probably the "Thule" mentioned by the Irish monk, Dicuil, around the year 825, that was described as an island with a frozen sea to the north of it. The Icelandic chronicler, Ari the Learned, believed that the Celtic monks fled the island when the Norse arrived permanently. But Celtic Christians were among the first Norse settlers of Iceland. Perhaps Irish monks even reached the shores of the New World.

ABOVE: St. Brendan, accompanied by a number of his followers, is said to have sailed the north Atlantic.

RIGHT: Legendary stories such as those in the *Life of St. Brendan the Navigator* tell of visits to otherworldly islands.

SAINTS' DISCIPLES

As in all religious traditions throughout the world, discipleship was important in Celtic Christianity. Traditional teaching involves a close personal relationship between teacher and student, and this was the case in the old Celtic monastic schools. Several saints who are well known in their own right, began their careers as disciples of famous saintly teachers. St. Aidan, for instance, was a disciple of St. David. Irish church history records a number of saints whose names show them to have been disciples of specific saints. In the Irish language, the epithet "Mael" signifies a person with the ecclesiastical tonsure and baptized by or dedicated to the tutelage of a certain saint. So there are Celtic saints with names such as Mael-putruicc, Mael-Columb, and Mael-Brighite. The cognomen Mael-putruicc means the protégé or disciple of St. Patrick, Mael-Columb that of St. Columba, and Mael-Brighite, St. Bridget.

ABOVE: St. Bridget feeding the starving dog.

Certain present day Celtic surnames such as Malcolm are derived from them, showing their bearers to be descendants of these ancient Celtic saints.

ST. PETROC

One of the chief saints of Cornwall is St. Petroc. He studied first at a monastery in south Wales, then spent twenty years at a monastery in Ireland, reading sacred and profane literature. Twenty years' study was the prescribed term of apprenticeship before a candidate became a Druid. After his studies, he went to Padstow, in Cornwall, where he is now revered as a patron saint. Each day, as a meditative exercise, Petroc stood in the sea chanting psalms from cock-crow till dawn. Such techniques, similar to St. Chad's nightly immersion in a holy well, are used as spiritual bodily exercises throughout Europe and Asia.

Although saints are ascribed wondrous powers, not all saints are infallible, and a story is told that during unseasonably rainy weather, Petroc swore that, on the next day, it would change. When the rain continued, the saint, having lost face, decided to go on a pilgrimage which became a mystic voyage in true Celtic style. Having visited Rome, and then Jerusalem, Petroc moved on toward India. He trudged to the seashore, where he fell asleep. When he awoke, he saw a huge silver bowl floating toward the shore. Leaving his sheepskin cloak and his staff, he entered it, and was taken across the sea. The silver bowl took him to a small island, where he lived for seven years, eating a single fish that, although consumed, was miraculously restored each day. When the seven years were up, the silver bowl reappeared, and took him back to the shore. There, his cloak and staff remained, having been guarded by a wolf during his absence. He took the wolf back with him to Cornwall and, in later years, no artist would make an image of St. Petroc without his wolf.

ST. TEILO

St. Teilo is one of the most important Welsh saints, around whom many legends are woven. *The Life of St. Teilo*, that tells some of his story, was in the form of a sermon read at each of his festivals at Llandaff Cathedral. In it, we are told that Teilo was son of Ensic and Guenhaf. Originally, he was called Elios, which is the Welsh version of Helios, the sun god's name. "His learning shone like the sun," but it is likely that he was born into a pagan family, and so bore a pagan name. Teilo was born at Penally, beyond Tenby in the most westerly part of Wales. Penally was the ancestral land of his family, the noble line of Cunedda Wledig, and in later times, the saint founded a church there, in which he was finally buried. In his young days, Teilo was taught by St. Dubricius, the man who is reputed to have crowned King Arthur. Later he went to Ty Gwyn, where he got to know St. David. He followed David from there to his new settlement at Glyn Rhoslyn, where St. David's cathedral now stands. But an Irish invasion and the consequent conflict led St. Teilo, along with St. David and St. Padarn to leave Wales on pilgrimage to Jerusalem.

In a great church in Jerusalem stood three chairs. Two were richly embellished with precious metals, while one was a plain chair of cedar wood. David and Padarn chose the fine chairs, while Teilo sat in the humble one. Then he was told that this was the chair from which Christ had taught, and so, from it, he must preach. Thus, his excellence as a religious teacher was made apparent to all. The Patriarch of Jerusalem gave David an altar of wonderful workmanship; to Padarn, a staff and a silken cope; and to Teilo, as the best preacher of all, a magnificent bell that had special virtues. This bell was later kept at his shrine in Llandaff Cathedral, along with his ritual comb and his bishop's miter.

When the three saints returned to Britain, Teilo went to Cornwall but he was soon forced to leave when, in the year 547, a devastating epidemic ravaged Britain. It was preceded by a strange portent in the form of a column of vapor that swept across the country. Every person and animal that came into contact with the vapor immediately became ill, and died. The yellow plague, as it was called, was rightly feared, and whole populations fled. Families and entire clans left their homesteads and sailed, if they could, to Brittany, where the pestilence was unknown. Among the many churchmen who joined the exodus was Teilo. He crossed the Channel from Cornwall to Brittany, and went to stay with St. Samson, at the monastery of Dôl, that he had founded in the year 544.

St. Teilo had a lot in common with St. Samson, "They came from the same district, they spoke the same language, and had both been educated by the same archbishop, Dubricius," the *Book of Llan Dâv* tells us. Teilo stayed with Samson for seven years and seven months. During his stay, he performed several great feats, including defeating a dragon and throwing it into the sea. Like most of the Celtic saints, Teilo seems to have had a close relationship with the natural world and the land on which he dwelt. Along with St. Samson, he planted an orchard of fruit trees that stretched three miles from Cai to Dôl. He also located a spring at Kerfeuntain. In certain Breton images, St. Teilo is shown riding upon a stag. When Teilo needed firewood, in the absence of oxen as draught animals, two stags volunteered to carry the wood to his monastery, and remained afterward to perform other chores.

After he returned again to Britain, Teilo was revered as a great wise man. Once, St. Cadoc asked seven fundamental questions to the seven wise men of his college at Llancarfan. When Teilo was asked the question, "What is the greatest wisdom in a man?" he replied, "To refrain from injuring another when he has the power to do so." Unlike St. Patrick and other saints who insisted on fasting to make God change his mind, Teilo taught his followers not to contend against God.

Around the year 577, Anglian forces defeated the Britons at the Battle of Deorham, and crossed the River Wye. The

ABOVE: The ruins of St. Teilo's church,
Llandeilo Llwydiarth,
Pembrokeshire.

Anglian advance into Wales was blocked at Llantilio Crossenny by the forces of Prince Iddon of Gwent, son of King Ynyr. According to ancient Celtic tradition, Iddon requested Teilo, who was his family priest, to lead his army spiritually before, and during, the conflict. Teilo and his assistants climbed a hill to view the battle and to sing curses against the Anglians, who were defeated. As a thanks offering, the prince granted Teilo the land on which the battle was won, including the hill, on which Teilo had a church constructed. In all, 37 churches are known to have been dedicated to St. Teilo in south and mid Wales.

When Teilo died at Llandeilo Fawr, in Carmarthenshire, there was an unseemly squabble for his body. The priests of Llandeilo Fawr said that he should be buried where he died; those from Llandaff asserted that he should be laid to rest in the cathedral that he had founded; while his relatives from Penally called for him to be brought back to lie in his ancestral soil there. It appears that the ancestral claim was given priority, and Teilo went back to Penally. However, the other claimants also pretended that they had the remains of this most powerful of saints, and that God, to satisfy the rival claimants, had miraculously multiplied the body into three identical corpses, one for each church. This explanation is not unusual in the case of famous saints, or other relics, such as the nails of the crucifixion, or the True Cross.

"The three supports of a godly man:
God and His gift of grace;
conscience itself; and the praise of
every wise and good man."

THE BARDIC TRIADS OF ST. PAUL

❧

CHAPTER VIII

Celtic Teachers and Saints

Celtic Teachers

There are a number of Celtic spiritual teachers who made substantial contributions to the Christian religion. Some were very successful and are recognized as saints, St. Patrick, for example, demonstrated his skill by setting up a new church and by converting Ireland to Christianity. Others were more controversial and were even condemned as heretics. In the bardic tradition, a spiritual teacher's lessons were often passed on in the form of threefold adages, called triads. The Bardic Triads of St. Paul are a well-known example.

PELAGIUS

The most controversial of all Celtic spiritual teachers was the British theologian, Morgan, better known by his Latin name, Pelagius, who was a respected religious teacher in Rome in the 380s. This was a time of turmoil, and Pelagius was forced to flee from Rome before the arrival of the Goths, who, under their Arian Christian king Alaric, finally sacked the city in the year 410. Before this happened, Pelagius emigrated to Carthage on the southern shores of the Mediterranean. However, the provincial city of Carthage was not as tolerant as Rome. In the year 411, his opponents in the church of Carthage managed to get his ideas condemned as heretical at a church council. The influential African theologian, St. Augustine, became an enemy of Pelagius, and wrote in condemnation of his ideas. Threatened with persecution for his beliefs, Pelagius then migrated to the Holy Land, where he was supported and protected by John, Bishop of Jerusalem. Pelagius died in the Holy Land in the 430s, but his theology lived on. The essence of his teachings was that evil and sin are external to the human being, and that through the exercise of free will we can gain salvation. His opponents, who were successful in having their ideas adopted by the mainstream church, asserted that salvation is dependent entirely upon the grace of God. They taught that, because everything is already preordained by God, all human efforts to attain perfection must fail.

Pelagius taught that, "We put in the first place, power; in the second, will; and in the third, manifestation. The first of these comes from God, who has given it to his own creatures. The other two... are related to the human condition, because they stream forth from the sources of the human will." Because of this natural source of energy, Pelagius taught, it is within human beings' own power to live a blameless life. This main principle of Pelagius, that we can have self-reliance in religious matters, and attain perfection, stems both from the Druidic and Stoic philosophies. In addition to his humane theology, Pelagius' teachings also addressed themselves to social justice, which did not enamor him to the ruling churchmen.

Pelagius was condemned by the mainstream church as a heretic, and his works were destroyed wherever they could be found. Despite the wholesale destruction of Pelagian literature as heretical, three quotations survive from an unnamed British follower of his who lived in Sicily. They ask the rhetorical questions of why the rich should possess more than the poor, "Should there be one law for the rich, and another for the poor?" Teachings telling of the equality of all have never been popular with rulers and, throughout time, religious teachers have been punished for expressing the truth that all people, rich and poor, were created equal by God. Because his ideas did not gain favor with the mainstream church, that adopted the north African theology of St. Augustine and his followers, and despite his goodwill, Pelagius was condemned as a bad man and hence he never became St. Morgan or St. Pelagius. In the 420s, despite attempts by north African religious theorists to suppress them, Pelagius' ideas were having an impact in his native Britain. Pelagian ideas were so widespread in Britain that, in the year 429, Germanus, Bishop of Auxerre, was requested by British church leaders to come to suppress them. Germanus' first anti-Pelagian visit seems to have been unsuccessful, for he was back in Britain in the 440s, on the same mission. The British king, Vortigern who, against all odds, kept Britain independent until the year 442, was a Pelagian Christian. Perhaps it was for this reason that later Christians, who viewed Pelagianism with horror, preferred to remember him as a bad king who brought in the Saxons, rather than a man who in fact did his best to maintain stability under impossible circumstances.

ST. PATRICK

A more successful teacher was St. Patrick, the apostle of Ireland, who is perhaps the most famous of all Celtic saints. There is a plethora of histories and legends about Patrick, but he seems to have been born at Bannaventa, in Britain, in the year 389. He was a son of a decurion, Calpurnius, and grandson of Potitus, the priest. At the age of six, Patrick was kidnaped by pirates, and sold as a slave in Ireland. After six years as a slave, Patrick escaped and left Ireland. He finally reached Gaul, and entered the monastery of Lerins. Around 416, Patrick was ordained a deacon at Auxerre by Bishop Amator. At the age of forty-five, he was consecrated bishop. Then he decided to return to Ireland to preach the Christian religion. In 444 he founded a monastery at Armagh, close to an important pagan royal settlement. He ordained over 300 bishops and 3,000 presbyters. In Connaught he also converted 12,000 laymen and, on one day, he baptized seven kings.

According to the *Lebhar na h'Uidre*, in the time of the Irish high king, Laoghaire, a folk-moot was convened at Tara to discuss religion, "when the fulness of the faith was settled with the men of Ireland." Then, the body of Irish laws known as Senchus Mór, "Great Antiquity," was revised to take the new religion into account. The high king and many of his followers remained pagan, but understood that the new religion must be accommodated in law. This revision, called Cain Patreuc "Patrick's Law" or Noi-fis "The Knowledge of the Nine," was made by a committee composed of three kings, three brehons, "lawyers," and three Christian bishops. The three kings were Laoghaire, High King of Ireland; Corc, King of Munster; and Daire, King of Ulster. Fergus the Poet, Dubhthach Maccu Lugair, and Ros, son of Trichem, were the three brehons, while Patrick, Benan, and

Cairnech were the priests. In this revision of the law, Patrick succeeded in replacing the Druids who would have participated in traditional law committees.

Sometimes the Celtic saints made magic weapons with which animals could be slain. We have already seen how St. Columba consecrated a magic spear, and we are told by the old chroniclers that Celtic saints sometimes killed wild or dangerous animals by means of prayer.

St. Patrick possessed a holy staff, Bachall Iesu, "The Staff of Jesus." According to legend, Jesus himself gave it to Patrick. With the power of this staff, St. Patrick expelled all the serpents from Ireland and, to this day, there are no snakes on the island. Some see this as a symbol of Patrick abolishing other religions from Ireland. The saint is reputed to have obtained even greater gifts from Jesus, wringing special concessions from God. He prayed to God that Irish people should be saved, even if their repentance was on the deathbed. Secondly, that unbelievers might never overcome him; and thirdly, that no Irish person should be left alive to suffer the reign of the Antichrist. So, we are told, he received the guarantee that Ireland would sink beneath the waves, like Atlantis, seven years before the Day of Doom.

LEFT: St. Patrick, patron saint of Ireland and possibly the most famous of all the Celtic saints.

ABOVE: St. Patrick was summoned by the Irish High King for lighting a fire on a hill at a ritual time when all fires should have been extinguished by law. This action enabled St. Patrick to assert his religious views to the members of the royal house.

The Tripartite Life of St. Patrick tells us that he also, unwisely, asked that he, and not God, should judge the Irish people on Judgment Day. An angel appeared to him and told him that, of course, this was not possible. Patrick then ascended the holy hill, called Hely, and began a fast against this decision, going without all drink or food until God changed his mind. After some days, he saw the angel again, offering him concessions. But these were not enough, and Patrick asserted, "I will not go from this place until I am dead, unless all things I have asked for are granted to me." Finally, almost at the edge of unconsciousness, he saw a vision in which the sky was filled with innumerable birds of all colors, that he took as the sign that God had given way, and granted his request. So he ceased his fast, which had lasted for forty days, and returned to his preaching.

Patrick's success in Ireland is all the more remarkable because others before him had failed. Patrick was not the first Christian to attempt to plant the new religion in Ireland, but "Not to Palladius, but to Patrick, God granted the conversion of Ireland." Palladius had been sent to Ireland in the year 431 by Pope Celestine, but was a total failure. Patrick died in the year 493, and is honored each year on March 17. His holy plant is the shamrock, whose three leaves he said symbolized the doctrine of the Holy Trinity.

OTHER ST. PATRICKS

As with many of the famous saints, there was more than one Patrick, and historians have often conflated their lives into that of a single person. Patrick MacCalpurn was author of the famous *Confession*, which shows that he is the authentic St. Patrick who established the Christian religion in Ireland. But there are others with whom St. Patrick is often confused. St. Sen Patrick for instance, was also a Briton, born somewhere on the Gower Peninsula near the present city of Swansea. However, he is so closely associated with the apostle of Ireland that it is said that he was told by the saint himself that they should enter heaven together. When Patrick died, he waited five months for Sen Patrick to die and, when he did, they entered heaven together as he had been promised. Another St. Patrick was the apostle's nephew, son of Sannan, the Deacon. Like Sen Patrick, he is often confused with his uncle.

There was also another St. Patrick, who was buried at Glastonbury Abbey. This could have been Patrick MacSannan, or the later abbot of Glastonbury who had the same name. As with many accounts of individual Celtic saints, Welsh traditions of St. Patrick differ from the Irish perceptions of their apostle. Another St. Patrick, Patrick ab Alfryd, from Anglesey may be the

ABOVE: The tales of the lives of other Patricks have been added to the legend of St. Patrick.

saint associated with the legend that, thirty years before the birth of St. David, St. Patrick had come to the holy place of Glyn Rhoslyn in west Wales, and had settled there. But an angel came and told St. Patrick to go west across the sea, and to convert the Irish to the Christian religion. The angel said that Glyn Rhoslyn would be settled by one, not yet born, who would come afterward – St. David.

ST. MAIDOC OF FERNS

Like St. Patrick, St. Maidoc of Ferns was a monk who attempted to wrest from God the assurance that no successor of his should be damned to go to hell. By his successors, he meant both those in his religious community and the members of his clan. To force God to agree to this unreasonable request, he went on hunger strike. After a fast lasting for fifty days, Maidoc, like Patrick, saw a vision that convinced him that God had granted his request. The attitude of Patrick and Maidoc came from the ancient Irish custom where an aggrieved individual could go on hunger strike against a lord or king until his grievances were addressed. The hunger strike remains part of the Irish political repertoire today. However, this coercive attitude is in complete contrast with the approach of the Welsh saint, Teilo who, in *The Stanzas of the Hearing* tells us, "It is not good to contend against God."

ABOVE: Farmyard chickens decorate an illuminated manuscript. Details of everyday life often featured in the work of Celtic monks.

SAINTLY CURSES

Celtic saints were men of their times, and therefore many of them did not abstain from killing either through physical means or through prayer and curses. In pagan times, the clan Druid was the official who performed the task of ritually cursing the enemies of the chief. Whenever an oath was sworn, or a contract made, the official Druid had to be present to oversee the business, and to curse anyone who should go back on his, or her, word. As Druidism was replaced by Christianity, or individual Druids were converted, the new Christian priests took over the social and legal, as well as the religious, functions. As with the Druids before them, the clan priest had the duty to curse the enemies of the king, and there are recorded instances of this. In Ireland, during a war between the Clan Niall and King Diarmuid, Mac Cearboil, the Christian king, was accompanied by a Druid who cursed and used magic against his foes. The warriors of the opposing clan were accompanied by a Christian priest who used his own powers to counter those of the royal Druid. The real power of the Celtic clergy is recalled by the maxim ascribed to St. Geraint, king and martyr, by the Welsh text, *The Sayings of the Wise*:

> "Hast thou heard the saying of Geraint,
> Son of Erbin, the just and experienced?
> 'Short-lived is the hater of the saints.'"

ᛞᛟ

RIGHT: A dramatic illustration by the nineteenth-century artist John Martin, showing an animated Druid cursing the enemies of his king.

ST. FINDCHUA

ABOVE: Celtic custom required that members of royalty, or their religious agents, would pronounce formal curses upon wrongdoers or enemies. The curse of Queen Macha against the men of Ulster made them feel the pangs of childbirth at the time of the province's greatest need of them.

ne of the most successful saints who used battle magic was St. Findchua, who served a number of provincial Irish kings. His career began when he was asked to curse the enemies of the King of Meath. He agreed and, we are told, as "sparks of fire burst forth from his teeth," the enraged saint led the Meath warriors into battle, "slaying their servants, burning their ships and making a cairn of their heads." The king was so pleased that the invaders had been exterminated that he gave a fortress to the saint, along with the lordly privileges that ownership of such a castle brought with it. The highest honor in the land, that the king's drinking horn should be brought to him once every seven years, was also granted to St. Findchua. In the next war, between Leinster and its enemies, the king still wanted his Druid to curse his foes. However, the Druid informed the king that he was too old to perform the rite, and St. Findchua was summoned in his place. The saint again went into a battle frenzy, called "the wave of godhead," and led the Leinstermen to victory. Next, the king of Munster used the services of the battling monk against the Ulstermen, riding in his chariot with his staff in his hand. Again, leading the army, St. Findchua was victorious, and afterwards was given the epithet "The Slaughterous Hero."

ST. FECHIN

he distinction between curses and supplications to God was not very well defined in ancient Celtia. The preface to *The Hymn of St. Colman* tells of a prayer to God, conducted by a holy man, that was effectively a curse. In the year 637, because of overpopulation, Ireland could not support its people. At an assembly convened by the Irish kings, Blathmac and Diarmidh, it was agreed to restrict the amount of land that could be farmed legally and, in addition, to ask God, through prayer, "to reduce the number of the lower class, so that the rest might live comfortably." The assembly asked St. Fechin of Fore to conduct the petition to God. He did so, and the yellow plague appeared in Ireland. God, it seems, answered the prayers, but in such a way that the brunt of the epidemic was borne by the upper class, for both kings and the saint promptly caught the plague and then died.

ST. FINNIAN

Although they were pious, and often stern men, this did not mean that at least some of the Celtic saints lacked a sense of humor. Celtic saints and Druids were not always at odds with one another. They could even share jokes. An Irish story tells how one day St. Finnian, "The Master of the Saints," was sitting on the ground, when Fracan, a Druid, came to him. They started to talk, and

Finnian asked Fracan where he got his wisdom, from heaven or earth. "Test me, and find out," answered Fracan. St. Finnian then asked the Druid if he could tell him where he would be resurrected, to which Fracan answered, "in heaven, of course." St. Finnian stood up, and asked him to try again. Fracan saw that the priest was not talking about resurrection after death, but resurrection from a sitting to a standing position. Despite the joke played upon him, this was where Fracan began to teach, and was finally buried.

ST. TALHAIARN

According to Celtic tradition, all actions can be sanctified by opening and closing prayers. They dedicate the work, or event, to the divine, bringing protection and empowerment to the participants. The following ancient prayer is said before each sitting of the Gorsedd Morganwg, the bardic sessions of Glamorgan, in south Wales. Composed 1,500 years ago by the priest-bard Talhaiarn, the domestic chaplain of Emrys Wledig (Aurelius Ambrosianus), the prayer calls upon God to give wisdom and understanding to the participants:

"God, impart strength;
And in that strength, reason;
And in reason, knowledge;
And in knowledge, justice;
And in justice, the love of it;
And in that love, love of everything;
And in the love of everything,
the love of God."

༺༒༻

CHAPTER IX

The Celtic Saints and Nature

Many of the legends that surround the Celtic saints show evidence of an intimate relationship with nature. This can take the form of delight in both the beauty of the natural world and in the wonder of human existence. A fascination and an intimacy with nature deepen the saints' belief in God. Animals also play an important part in the Celtic harmony with nature. Various animals serve as omens to the saints in pointing to sites for the foundation of new churches. A number of saints take on a protective role towards the animals, often saving them from the threat of hunters.

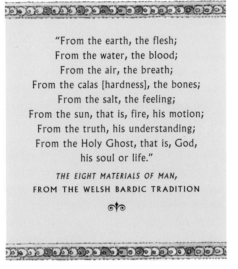

"From the earth, the flesh;
From the water, the blood;
From the air, the breath;
From the calas [hardness], the bones;
From the salt, the feeling;
From the sun, that is, fire, his motion;
From the truth, his understanding;
From the Holy Ghost, that is, God,
his soul or life."

THE EIGHT MATERIALS OF MAN,
FROM THE WELSH BARDIC TRADITION

ST. FINGAR

A number of Celtic saintly histories describe how an insight into the nature of the world led the individual to a belief in God. St. Fingar's conversion came from his profound encounter with the inexpressible beauty of existence. His biographers tell us that he was the son of an Irish king, Clyto. As the result of a coup, he and his brothers were expelled from Leinster, and sailed to Brittany. It was there that Fingar was given land upon which to settle. When he was out hunting one day, on his new estate, Fingar killed a stag and butchered it. He loaded the stag onto his horse and then went looking for a spring where he could wash the blood from himself. He was unable to find a spring, however, and he thrust his spear into the ground where, miraculously, a spring of fresh water spurted forth. He was washing himself in the new waters, when he saw his own reflection and was suddenly impressed with his own handsomeness. Realizing what a fine fellow he was, he understood that his beauty came from God. So, he resolved then and there to devote his beauty to his creator, who had brought him into being. He built a hut next to the spring, and there resolved to live the rest of his life as a holy hermit.

LEFT: Angels attain the Holy Grail, the ultimate goal of Christian saints.

ST. AILBE

 he story of St. Ailbe gives us an insight into the relationship between wild nature and Celtic spirituality. Ailbe's father, Olchais, loved a maidservant who worked in the service of Cronan, chief of the Eliach of Tipperary. When the girl became pregnant, Olchais ran away, fearing that he would be punished. So, when the baby was born and there was no father there to support him, Cronan ordered that the baby should be abandoned behind a rock, out in the open country, and left to die. But the baby was discovered there by a she-wolf that suckled and sustained him until he was found by a man named Lochan. Lochan called the baby Ailbe, after the ail, "rock," where he was found. When he had grown, Ailbe was fostered with some British people from Wales who had settled in the vicinity. As a boy, Ailbe was fascinated by nature, and in particular, by the starry heavens. On one occasion, he was talking to himself, asking the eternal question, "Who could have made these lights? Who set them in their places, and ordered the sun and moon to run their courses? O that I might know him!" At that very moment, a Christian priest was passing by and, overhearing him, decided to take him for baptism and instruction in religion. He became a monk as a result of this, and finally rose to the rank of bishop. St. Ailbe's relationship with nature was not broken by his elevation to high rank, however. Once, while at a wolf hunt, the pursued beast sought refuge beneath his cloak. The bishop refused to allow the huntsmen to kill the wolf, saying, "Ah, my friend! When I was feeble and friendless, you protected me, and now I will do the same for you."

ST. MELANGELL

T he most potent instance of Celtic harmony with nature is the story of St. Melangell, the daughter of an Irish king. Renouncing her status as princess for the religious life, she became a nun, but despite this, was ordered to marry the man of her father's choice. In order to escape this forced marriage, she fled eastward across the Irish Sea and settled at Pennant, in Wales. She is considered a protectress because of an incident that took place during a hunt in the year 604, conducted by the prince of Powys, Brochwel Ysgithrog. While his hounds were chasing a hare, the prince came across Melangell, praying devoutly in a bramble thicket. The hare was hiding inside the sleeve of Melangell's garment, and looked out at the dogs. Prince Brochwel called to the dogs to catch the hare, but they retreated in fear from the saint, and ran off. The prince had never experienced anything like this before, so he asked the woman her name, and what she was doing there. After she had told him, Brochwel acknowledged her holy power as "a handmaiden of the true God, and most sincere worshiper of Christ."

Because God had enabled her to protect the wild hare from the vicious hunting dogs, Brochwell gave her the lands across which his hunt had come. After that, the lands of Pennant Melangell became a sanctuary under her guardianship. She lived there for another thirty-seven years, during which time no animal was killed on her land. The wild animals living there became tame and humans too, could claim sanctuary from persecution at Pennant Melangell. After her death, St. Melangell became the tutelary saint of hares, which are called *wyn Melangell*, "Melangell's Lambs." To kill a hare in Melangell's parish was an act of sacrilege. St. Melangell is recognized today as the Celtic patroness of animals and the natural environment. According to the Celtic Christian philosophy, because the natural environment is the manifestation of God's will on earth, those who destroy it are not only threatening the continuance of all life on earth, but also going counter to "the protection and favor of the Creator."

ABOVE: St. Melangell became the guardian saint of hares.

RIGHT: The St. Neot window in the church of that name in Cornwall.

ST. NEOT

St. Neot, after whom the English town of St. Neot's in Huntingdonshire is named, came from Glastonbury to live on the remote and inhospitable Bodmin Moor, in Cornwall. It is likely that he was an illegitimate son of an Anglo-Saxon king, probably Ethelwulf, who, after serving as a military man, gave up violence and became a monk. St. Neot was a saint who lived in harmony with the natural world, and had power over animals. During his prayers, he was disturbed by the croaking of crows, so he ordered them to go to the nearby ancient earthwork and stay there until he had finished. Once, when his oxen were stolen, he summoned wild deer to his aid, and harnessed them to the plow instead. On another occasion, St. Neot was praying by his holy well, when a hunted deer came to him for protection. When the hounds came to him, Neot stopped them from attacking the deer, and the huntsman, moved by the experience, gave up his profession and became a monk. He gave his hunting horn to the church at Bodmin, where it remained for many centuries. After his death, Neot was buried at St. Neot's in Cornwall, but in the year 974, his body was stolen by Earl Alric of Huntingdonshire, and brought to the town of Eynesbury, that now bears the name of St. Neot.

ST. CARANNOG

Bird omens were deemed highly significant by the pagan Celts, and the tradition was continued by the Christian priests. The story is told of St. Carannog, who decided to settle at Carhampton, in Somersetshire. Like all the early Celtic priests, Carannog was self-sufficient and he immediately began work. He borrowed a spade from a local farmer, and dug the foundations of a church. Needing a pastoral staff, he selected an appropriate piece of wood. While he was sitting, carving the staff head, a wood pigeon came down from a tree, picked up some of the wood shavings, and flew off with them. Seeing this as an omen, Carannog followed the bird, and discovered that she had taken all of the shavings to a certain place, to build her nest. So, he abandoned the already-dug foundations, and erected a church at the place that the wood pigeon had selected for him.

ABOVE: The Celtic saints believed in the ability of birds to carry messages from God.

RIGHT: Legend tells us both of St. Neot instructing deer to help him and of his protecting them from huntsmen.

ANIMALS AND THE CELTIC CHURCH

The boar is a prognostic animal which appears in many episodes of Celtic myth, where it is said to have originated in the otherworld. Often, the boar is only the outward form of a transformed being, either a deity or a human. To the pre-Christian Celts, the wild pig was the holy animal of the earth goddess, Cerridwen and the god of the secular clan, Teutates. As the goddess' animal, the sow is a symbol of the earth's limitless fecundity, because she gives birth to a large litter of piglets at one time and is fertile for many years. Also like the earth, the sow devours her own dead young. In the autumn, wild swine trample the muddy earth, and in so doing, plant the fallen seeds in the ground. The boar who, unlike the sow, lives alone, symbolizes the power of self-reliance in human society. This is exemplified by the hero, who is the warrior on the physical plane, and the monk, his counterpart in the spiritual world. However, in Celtic legends, the boar usually takes second place to the sow as a holy animal. Apart from their economic uses, both domesticated and wild pigs were held in respect by the early Celtic priests. Like the saint whom they emulated, Celtic monks of the ascetic cultus of St. Anthony of Egypt were enthusiastic swineherds. The Christian pig tradition of St. Anthony merged seamlessly with the earlier traditions of the devotees of Cerridwen and Teutates. Celtic monks believed that St. Anthony's pigs were special because they were able to discover lost or hidden sacred objects.

These holy pigs were especially successful in the search for buried bells. Whenever they were discovered, these mysterious holy bells were held in great regard for they possessed the power of warding off the evil spirits that cause fires and storms.

There are a number of Celtic foundation legends involving swine. The prolific sixth century church founder, St. Dyfrig, sometimes known by his latinized name, St. Dubricius, was a land owner in his own right. His estate, Inis Ebrdil, was in south Wales. When Dyfrig decided to found his own monastery, he traveled through his lands to find the best place to build it. In a meander of the River Wye, on thorny land, he encountered a wild white sow with her piglets, which he took as the omen. There Dyfrig erected the monastery that he called Mochros (the swine-moor). Around the year 660, St. Arbogast, whose name means "Boar Spirit," founded the monastery of Ebersmunster in the Forêt de Hageuenau, in Alsace, now in eastern France, according to the same swine omen. Other beasts also gave omens to those who were seeking them. After giving up a life of violence, King Gwynllyw the Warrior, "St. Wooloo," decided to build a church in expiation. He traveled his lands in search of an omen. Finally, when he saw a white ox, with one black spot on its forehead, standing on a high point in the land, he knew that was the place for the new church.

Some animal omens were more complex, involving first an apparition, or dream, which pointed out the animal to the dreamer. When he was about to found a new church on his own land at Llwyn in Ceinmeirch, St. Ieuan Gwas Padrig, a disciple of St. Patrick, was advised by an angel not to build his church there. Instead, he was to travel southward until he saw a roebuck. At the place where he saw it rise, he should construct the new church.

At Cerrig y Drudion, Ieuan saw the predicted roebuck, and there he made the church. Similarly, around the year 880, the Empress Richardis, consort of the holy Roman emperor, Charles the Fat, was staying at the monastery of Mont-Sainte-Odile in Alsace. One night, an angel appeared to her in a dream. It told her that she should journey southward from the holy mountain until she encountered a she-bear with her cub, standing on a rock, which was the holy place which she was destined to hallow. Following the angelic instructions, Richardis traveled due south across country, until she encountered the predicted bear. There, over the bear's rock, she built the Abbey of Andlau where, to this day, a statue of a bear stands in the crypt. This stone bear faces a trap door in the crypt floor, beneath which lies the very rock upon which the bear stood.

Like the sow and the cow, the roebuck and the bear were holy animals associated with certain pre-Christian Celtic deities. According to Celtic folk tradition, the stag is a royal beast. An old Irish legend associates the deer with divining who should be king, "a fawn with golden lustre will enter the assembly, and the son who will catch the fawn is he that will take the kingdom." The Northern Tradition has strong connections with animal powers; whether in the pagan tradition, or under the aegis of Christianity, the same powers have affected human actions. In the pagan tradition, many deities have their animal parallel. Here, the stag is the beast of the horned lord of the animals, Cernunnos, and the Romano-British deity, Cocidius, god of hunting. Similarly, Vosegos, the god who personifies the Vosges mountains in eastern France, is shown accompanied by a stag. Dea Arduinna, the Celtic goddess of the Ardennes, is depicted seated on a wild boar, while the she-bear is sacred to the bear goddess, Artio. Close to the ancient shrine of Artio, the city of Bern, now the capital of Switzerland, was founded by a knight after a supernatural hunting incident. In the twelfth century, a knight beheld a miraculous apparition of a bear. This omen was blessed by the church and emperor, and the city was built. Bears have been kept in a special bear pit at Bern continuously to this day. They are the "luck" of the city. Some of these animal deities appear in a Christian context transformed into saints, such as St. Arbogast, while Celtic saints, such as Teilo, are sometimes shown riding on a stag.

Combinations of animals were sometimes taken as portents of things to come. The omens given to Sant; the bees, stag, and fish, told him of the characteristics of the son that he was about to father – St. David. According to the *Cognatio de Brychan*, St. Brychan was given a similar omen, when his master, Drychan, saw a

portentous combination of animals, "and whilst he lay awake, a certain boar came from the wood and stood by the banks of the River Yscir, and there was a stag behind it in the river and also a fish under the belly of the stag, which then portended that Brychan should be happy in abundance of wealth."

Celtic priests sometimes used animals, like oxen, more actively in selecting the sites for new churches. When the Welsh Celtic saints, Cadoc, Dunwyd, and Tathan wanted to build a new church, they loaded their building materials onto a wagon drawn by a pair of oxen. They did not drive the oxen, but allowed them to pull the wagon according to their own will. The saints decided that where the oxen stopped, that would be their church site. Eventually, they did stop at an open high point between two woods, and this is where the church was then built.

ST. HOIERNIN

 ccasionally, abnormal hunting incidents could serve as omens. The story of the genesis of St. David comes into this category. A number of holy places, such as the sites of forgotten saints' graves, or locations for new towns, were divined by hunted deer. A typical instance took place in Brittany, during a hunt in the year 550, when Conmore, Count of Poher, witnessed unexpected behavior from the stag he was pursuing. Without warning, the beast stopped, and his hounds declined to kill it. It was a miracle, because the place was found to be the lost grave of Saint Hoiernin, at which the stag had stopped to gain the protection of the saint. Conmore ordered a church to be built there in commemoration of the miracle.

ST. ENDELIENTA

St. Endelienta, a Cornish holy woman, was reputed to live on a diet of cow's milk alone. Nicholas Roscarrock, in his *Lives of the Saints*, tells how she found the site of her own grave:

"when she perceived the day of her death drew
nigh, she entreated her friends after
her death to lay her dead body on a bed,
and to bury her there where certain young
stots, bullocks and calves of a day old should
of their own accord draw her, which being
done they brought her to a place which at that
time was a mirey waste ground, and a great
quagmire on the top of a hill, where
in time after there was a church built dedicated
to her."

❧

ABOVE: According to tradition, deer can act as omens to indicate who is king or where a church is to be founded.

The Landscape of the Saints

Holy Places of the Saints

In traditional Celtic society, the ancestral holy places, the collective shrines of the community, were maintained by the families who legally owned them. According to Celtic common law, land could not be bought and sold, only inherited. Any man who became a priest in the Celtic church maintained his family's legal rights over its inherited shrines. When a family, or its leading man, was converted to the Christian religion, the sacred places were also converted for the use of the new religion. Many of the ancient monasteries in Celtic lands are on such sites, but a significant number of Christian sacred places were founded in areas not previously recognized as holy. The accounts of the lives of Celtic saints contain many instances of geomancy, where holy places were located by omens, or special techniques were used to demarcate sacred ground.

Historically, these techniques can be traced back to both pagan Celtic tradition, and to the classical methods used by the Roman college of surveyors, known as the Agrimensores. Often, in the context of the Celtic saints, these events are presented as miraculous or the saint is shown as outwitting the donor by supernatural means. For

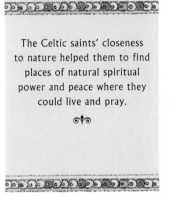

The Celtic saints' closeness to nature helped them to find places of natural spiritual power and peace where they could live and pray.

example, St. Hoiernin was a British immigrant to Brittany, who asked the local lord at Quelen for some land for his monastic settlement. The lord answered that he could have as much land for his minihi, or estate, as he could make a dyke around in a single day. Hoiernin walked around a large area, trailing his staff along the ground. According to legend, this act miraculously constructed a ditch and bank around the area. The saintly abbot called Gwyddno, or Goueznou, also accomplished the same feat. Whilst Count Conmore was out hunting, near Brest, he met Gwyddno, who asked him if he could have some land for a monastery. Like St. Hoiernin, he was told that he could have as much land as he could enclose in a day. Accompanied by his son, Majan, Gwyddno took a fork to mark the boundary. The fork miraculously dug a ditch delineating the new monastic grounds, that extended for six miles. Sometimes, the boundary was defined by the walk of a holy animal. St. Elian had a pet doe, and Caswallon gave him as much land as his deer could walk around in one day.

LEFT: The Welsh pilgrims' path to Ffynnon Fair, opposite Bardsey Island.

SACRED WALKING

o the Celtic saints, the simple every-day necessity of walking along a road was a spiritual act. The Christian tradition has many references to spiritual walking along "the straight and narrow way," that symbolizes the devotee's adherence to the law of God. A traditional Gaelic maxim tells us, "He who will not take advice will take the crooked track." Being on the right track is a metaphor of the pilgrim's journey to paradise and the ancient Celtic trackways reflect this spiritual meaning in the material world. Some of the trackways by which the Celtic saints traveled are still walkable, and are named after the saints whose legends ensoul the landscape around them. There are monastic footpaths and tracks on Dartmoor, in western England, and in the Wicklow Mountains of Ireland. They are marked by unmistakable holy stopping places, such as isolated boul-ders, cairns, thorn trees, and stone crosses, at each of which the pious wayfarer would stop and say a prayer. These points were also established as waymarks that enabled the traveler to find his, or her, way. These old Celtic monks' routes show a remarkably inti-mate knowledge of the landscape, for they have moderate gradients, avoid hill crests, and cross rivers at the best places.

In addition to everyday trackways for secular use, the Celtic saints made holy roads that linked sacred places. These were for the use of pilgrims and, on holy days, would have been walked ceremonially in procession. Such a holy road is Casan na Naomh (The Pathway of the Saints), that links Kilmakedar church with St. Brendan's Mountain, in County Kerry. This saints' road is a causeway over seven miles long, a major engineering work in its own right. The Irish road called The Track of St. Patrick's Cow is another. In Britain, the holy roads are attributed to St. Elen. As *The Dream of Maxen Wledig* tells us, "Elen bethought her to make high-roads from one town to another throughout the island of Britain. And the roads were made, and for this cause they are called the roads of Elen Luyddog."

ABOVE: When the wandering monks of Lindisfarne, seeking a grave for St. Cuthbert's body, came to Durham, they saw there a woman with the dun cow that they knew was the omen that showed the place where they should build their new church.

PILGRIMS' WAYS

ong and dangerous pilgrimages have always been an important element of Celtic Christian practice. They include the more significant, long distance pilgrimages across Europe to Rome or Santiago de Compostela and as far as the Holy Land, and more local ones, such as the Welsh pilgrimages to the holy island of Bardsey and the shrine at St. David's. Even more localized are sacred circuits. Pilgrims who undertake sacred circuits visit a series of specific holy places in a certain order. These sites may either be concentrated in a small area, or may be spread more widely, as stopping places along a route. On a sacred circuit, pilgrims visit a related series of sanctified places of different kinds, undergoing a wide variety of sacred experiences that cause a sequential change of consciousness. The most widespread Christian circuit in use today is the Stations of the Cross. Here, the pilgrim goes through a series of stopping places in sequence, each of which recalls an episode from the passion of Christ, culminating in his crucifixion. This walking spiritual exercise originated in the fifteenth century, but was a refinement of earlier artificial sacred landscapes. Whatever their specific religious theme, sacred circuits recall, in a limited area, the character of much longer pilgrimages.

Sacred circuits can be undertaken alone, as an individual meditation, but it is when they are performed collectively that they are at their most spiritually powerful. When performed singly, the circuit is called a round. Prayers are said and other appropriate rites are conducted at each stopping place. When a crowd of pilgrims do the circuit on the

ABOVE: The pilgrims' path at Nevern, Pembrokeshire, on the route between Holywell and St. David's.

patronal saint's day, this is known, in Ireland, as the saint's pattern, while in Brittany, it is called a pardon. One of the greatest sacred circuits still performed is held at Locronan, a few miles north of Quimper. The holy place recalls the Celtic saint, Ronan, otherwise known as Ruan, or Moruan, who came from Ireland. Ronan's pardon is known as La Tröménie, after the Breton *tro minihy*, "the monk's walk." Each year, at Locronan, a sacred walk takes place, covering 3.7 miles (6 km). Fasting, barefoot pilgrims visit a series of holy stopping places, including the holy hill on which St. Ronan's church stands, and a rock called Kador St. Ronan, "St. Ronan's Chair," which they walk round three times, praying. This is an arduous enough pilgrimage but, every six years, a much longer circuit is made. Called the Grand Troménie, it stretches for 8.7 miles (14km), along which barefoot, and fasting, devotees follow the ancient paths, trackways, and roads upon which St. Ronan used to walk. This sacred round follows the entire boundary of the saint's territory. It encompasses no fewer than forty-four holy stopping places, each of which is decorated with flowers during the Troménie.

The Troménie at Locronan is still long enough to be a strenuous undertaking, but most sacred circuits are now less demanding. One of the most complete examples of a smaller sacred circuit may be visited in Ireland, at Ballinavourney, in County Cork, where St. Gobnat is venerated. This sacred place contains a series of holy places in a remarkably small area. The first stopping place, at the entrance to the shrine, is at a modern image of the saint. Next, pilgrims visit an ancient holy well where cups are provided for those who wish to drink the curative waters. Then, the pilgrim enters a circular stone enclosure. This is the remains of a prehistoric build-ing known as St. Gobnat's house. In the middle stands a stone pillar, upon which each pilgrim scratches a cross, using a stone picked up from the floor. After St. Gobnat's house, the pilgrim enters the churchyard, that holds the ruins of an

ABOVE: A statue of St. Gobnat in Ballyvourney, Co. Cork.

ancient church, next to a modern one. Entering the ruined church, the pilgrim kneels at the eastern end, and scribes a cross upon a stone there. After this, the round goes to a another holy well, adjoining the south wall of the church. The next stopping place is an earthen mound, close to the churchyard gate, known as St. Gobnat's grave. It is customary for the devotee to crawl around it on their knees. Those who came on crutches or with walking sticks, but who no longer need them because of the curative power of St. Gobnat, leave them on the mound in thanksgiving. After the grave has been circled, pilgrims go through a stile below the churchyard, to visit the third, and final, holy well to drink the waters and thereby end the round.

St. Gobnat's shrine is a particularly fine example of the type of holy stopping places that comprise the typical sacred circuit. Each of them has some specific connection with the life, or legend, of the saint, and thereby has its own powers which can be drawn upon, by the pilgrim, for his, or her, spiritual sustenance. Even whole districts can be considered wholly sacred and be ascribed special powers, because of their saintly connections. In the area around Loch Maree, in the region of Gaerloch, Scotland, there are many of the holy stopping places of the saint known variously as St. Maree, St. Maelrubha and even "the god Mourie." In 1774, the traveler, Thomas Pennant wrote how "if a traveller passes any of his resting-places, they never neglect to leave an offering... a stone, a stick, a bit of rag." Certain of these hills are held in reverence to this day. It is said of the hill called Claodh Maree, that nobody can commit suicide, or otherwise injure him- or herself, within view of this place.

Celtic Holy Places

As well as consecrating stopping places for prayer on sacred trackways, some of these cross-bearing stones were boundary markers. St. Gwyddno who, like St. Kevin, St. Columba, and many of the other Celtic saints, kept women out of their holy places, set up a standing stone on his land. It marked the point beyond which women were not to pass. Ancient Celtic tradition possessed a system of taboos called geis, that included holy spirit places that only divine, or sacred, persons were considered pure enough to enter. In pagan times, these were marked by standing stones, and in Christian times, by crosses. Standing stone crosses are the most characteristic artefacts of Celtic Christianity. Many of the earlier ones were older stones reconsecrated to the Christian religion by the addition of a cross. Later ones were custom made slabs carved with wheel crosses and finally, after three or four centuries, free standing stone crosses were made. Successive generations of stone-masons progressively enlarged and elaborated these wheel-headed stone crosses, culminating in the great high crosses of Ireland, such

ABOVE: The Cross of Muiredach is an example of an elaborate wheel-headed stone cross, to be found at the ancient monastic settlement at Monasterboice.

as those that still stand today at many of the ancient monastic settlements, such as Ahenny, Castledermot, Clonmacnois, Moone, and Monasterboice.

In Ireland, there also remain a number of very ancient altars, that are the forerunners of the later Celtic high crosses. Known as leachta, they are rectangular drystone structures about the size of a church altar. Surmounting each leacht is a stone slab, into which is set an upright stone cross. On the top surface of most leachta are large, loose pebbles, which people rotate as they say prayers and invocations. The crosses on top of each leacht resemble the ancient pillar stones that were set up on pagan Celtic burial places. The exact nature of these places of the Celtic saints is still a matter for debate. Their Irish name comes from the Latin word for a bed, lectus, which is what graves are sometimes called in the Celtic realms. Fortunately, they are all considered so sacred that no archaeologist has been allowed to dig into them to see what is inside. So, it is not known whether they are the tombs of Celtic saints, but the leachta remain as holy stopping places at which devout people can meditate and pray.

ST. SAMSON

In the transition from pagan to Christian beliefs, several of the Celtic saints are known to have converted standing stones into Christian monuments by carving crosses upon them. The chronicler Tirechan, in his *The Acts of Patrick*, preserved in *The Book of Armagh*, describes how a rock at Lia na Manach, near the church of Kilmore, in County Mayo, was dedicated to Christianity by St. Patrick, who cut a cross upon it. But of all the cross cutters, St. Samson was clearly the most active. In the *Life* of this early sixth century saint, we are told of an incident when he cut a cross upon a stone. On his travels from Wales to Brittany, he was passing through a district of Cornwall called Tricurius. As he traveled along, he came across a group of villagers conducting a ritual at what Samson's biographer called an "abominable image," that is, a standing stone. Samson stopped the ceremony and rededicated the stone to Christian use, by incising a cross upon it.

The Tricurius stone was not the only one altered by the hand of St. Samson, for numerous stones throughout Wales, southwest England, and Britanny bear his name. Among his named stones are those called *Ffust Samson*, or "Samson's Flail," Samson's Jack, and Carreg Samson. All of these are in Glamorgan, south Wales. Other

ABOVE: St. Samson carried the Christian message across the sea from Wales to Brittany.

parts of Wales also have megaliths named Carreg Samson, including a standing stone on the mountainside at Llandewi Brefi, two groups of standing stones, or cromlechs in north Pembrokeshire, and a stone cross that stands near the church porch at Llanbadarn Fawr, close to Aberystwyth. In south Wales, Samson's Christianized megaliths mark the route of his journey from Llantwit Major to Dôl in Brittany, where there is a megalith called St. Samson's miter. Another Samson stone stands at Penvern, Côte-du-Nord, next to which a chapel of the saint was built between 1575 and 1631. At Berriew, in Powys, is a standing stone dedicated to the early Celtic missionary, St. Beuno. The church and chapel at the shrine of St. Beuno, at Clynnog Fawr, on the Lleyn peninsula, stand upon megaliths which may once have been components of stone rows or circles. One of the stones emerges through the nave floor, while others form the foundations. There are many other ancient standing stones throughout the Celtic realms that bear crosses carved by unknown Celtic priests.

As in the earlier days, when the Druids were the clan priests, Celtic Christians acknowledged animal omens. Just as the Druids had done, the Christian priests saw unusual animal behavior as indicating new sacred places, appropriate for new churches, monasteries, and burial places. Various animals are known to have done this. They range from insects to the largest mammals. A Breton legend tells how, on one occasion, St. Samson was wandering through the countryside with his disciples, seeking a suitable location for a new religious settlement. When they came to a bramble bush growing over a spring, Samson pointed out a number of locusts which had settled upon it. Immediately, he recognized this as an omen, for the Latin name for locust, *locusta*, can also be interpreted as the instruction *locus sta!*, "stay here." So, the settlement that later became the monastery of Dôl was set up at that location.

ST. COLLEN

St. Collen is remembered at Glastonbury, in western England, and Llangollen, in north Wales. Collen, who came from Porth Hantwn, the present day Southampton, had an anchorite's cell on the side of Glastonbury Tor. The tor is a pagan holy hill dedicated to Gwynn ap Nudd, lord of the kingdom of faery, and guardian of the gates of Annwn, the underworld.

One day, Collen admonished two men for talking about Gwynn ap Nudd, and was told that he would have to answer for his impudence. Later, a messenger arrived, dressed in red and blue. He told Collen that he must climb to the top of the tor and visit the palace of Gwynn ap Nudd, to explain himself. Collen would not go, and on the next day, the messenger returned, and insisted that Collen come, or it would be the worse for him. Collen took some holy water, and climbed the tor. On top, he saw a fine castle. Entering the castle, his ears were charmed by the finest music he had ever heard. Beautiful maidens and handsome youths, dressed in red and blue, escorted him to the great hall, where Gwynn was seated on a golden throne. Gwynn offered the saint wonderful food and drink, but he declined to eat the faery fare. Gwynn asked Collen whether he knew what the red and blue clothing symbolized, and Collen told him, rightly, that the red signifies hot, while the blue means cold. At that, Collen got out the holy water and sprinkled it around the castle, and over Gwynn and his servants. Immediately, the vision faded, and Collen found himself sitting on the grassy summit of Glastonbury Tor. Later, a church was built there in place of the spectral castle of Gwynn.

SAINTS' HOLY WELLS

The great Romanized Celtic water shrines at Bath, Buxton, and Lydney gradually went out of use after the fall of Britain. But the veneration of healing and holy waters was not abolished, for holy wells remain plentiful in all of the Celtic lands, and most of the Celtic saints have holy wells dedicated to them. The wells are not deep, stone-lined shafts but rather, natural springs, marked and protected by stone structures or buildings. Many resemble smaller versions of the great Celto-Roman sanctuaries. They often have provision for drinking, bathing, contemplation, and worship. It is probable that the vast majority of these holy wells were venerated before the introduction of the Christian religion. They were rededicated by the Celtic saints whose name they bear. The attributes of the indwelling spirits of the holy wells were transferred to the saints whose names they now bear. Most of these wells have waters reputed to heal specific ills.

Water taken from saints' wells on certain days is considered to be particularly powerful. In addition to the individual saint's own day, the most auspicious days are New Year's Day, Palm Sunday, and Ascension Day. In many places, devotees make a pilgrimage to the holy well on the saint's day, aware of the empowerment that they receive by drinking the saint's water on that day. In Cornwall, there were

ABOVE: St. Gwenfrewi's Well in Holywell, North Wales. The spring rose at the point where her severed head fell.

once official pilgrimages to the holy wells at Gulval, Nantswell, and Roche. Pilgrims visited the sanctified wells on the eve of the saint's day, and spent the night there in prayer and contemplation. After the vigil, at sunrise, they took part in the ceremony called bowsenning, where they were immersed in the healing waters in order to receive the blessing of the saint. Similar rites are observed in Brittany and Ireland to this day.

ST. GWENFREWI

St. Gwenfrewi, known in English as St. Winefride, and formerly patroness of Wales, has the most powerful of all British holy wells dedicated to her. Gwenfrewi is one of those saints who, after being killed, was miraculously restored to life. Her story took place on Midsummer's Day. Left alone in her parents' house, she was visited by a young man, called Caradog. While out hunting, he had felt thirsty and stopped at the house to ask for water. But when he saw the beautiful young woman, his interest turned from drink to sexual matters. She did not want his attentions, and fled to a chapel nearby, where St. Beuno was praying. Enraged, Caradog pursued her to the chapel door, where he cut off her head with his sword. Where the head fell, the rock opened and a spring rose up. St. Beuno, hearing the conflict, ran to her aid and, seeing the severed head, set it again on the body of Gwenfrewi. St. Beuno then cursed Caradog, who melted away to nothingness. After her miraculous resurrection, she traveled from holy place to holy place, finally returning to St. Beuno's church at Holywell, where she set up a convent of nuns. Later, she moved to another nunnery at Gwytherin.

She died and was buried there on All Souls' Day, fifteen years after the miraculous restoration of her head. Her relics were taken with great ceremony to Shrewsbury Abbey in 1138, at which point, her bones having left Wales, St. David was appointed as patron of that nation in her stead. Her shrine at Holywell, in north Wales, is the greatest holy well of Britain, with the most copious natural spring in the island, reckoned among the seven wonders of Wales. St. Winefride's Well is still one of the most important pilgrimage places in Great Britain. It is, in reality, far more than a well, being a holy water shrine, contained within a two story late Gothic building. A small chapel extends from the hillside, while below it is a polygonal well chamber from which the holy waters flow. In the base of the well chamber are some curious stones that bear red marks symbolizing the blood of Gwenfrewi.

The Welsh bard, Tudur Aled, who lived between the years 1465 and 1525, wrote a *cywydd* in praise of St. Gwenfrewi, telling of the red stones that lie in her well. It is a complex, symbolic poem, drawing on the imagery of the waters of life, the well, and the blood of Gwenfrewi and Christ. It weaves a typically Celtic integrated religious teaching that links the physical world with the symbolic and holy:

"In the earth, red-marked stones,
Musk and balm within the world,
A pure white stone with a pure place,
Stones marked with the blood of a white neck,
Which mark endures forever?
The band of her blessed blood.
A shower of tears like rose-hips,
Droplets of Christ,
from the wounds of the Cross;

It is good for a man's body –
To accept tears of blessed water;
Bloody droplets, like water and wine,
Bringing miracles of laughter.
The laughter of the seething sweet water
Is a sign of health – the bells of the water.
A burning stream from the fiery foam,
The powerful support of the Holy Ghost,
The waters of baptism are
the life support of the world,
It is the fountain of the oil of faith."

☙❧

Holywell is unique in Great Britain because of its unbroken continuity as a traditional sacred place, probably since pre-Christian times, and certainly through the religious upheavals of the Reformation into the present day. In the medieval period, it was under the control of monastic orders and, uniquely, the holy well was spared destruction during the Reformation. Although the sacred images were destroyed, a resident priest remained guardian of the holy well. This priestly guardianship continued until 1688, when protestants ransacked the chapel and expelled the priest. But even after that, people continued to visit the well and, in 1851 and 1887, successive popes granted indulgences to pilgrims who made visits to the well. Unlike St. Gwenfrewi's holy well, her tomb shrine at Shrewsbury was desecrated during the Reformation, and her bones were scattered and lost.

Miraculous springs rising at the places where a severed head fell are also spoken of in the legends of St. Jutwara, St. Noyala, and St. Tegiwg. In the saintly legend of St. Tegiwg, St. Beuno also restores the severed head of the princess at the place where her holy well, Ffynnon Digwg, rose.

ST. TRILLO

 t Llandrillo-yn-Rhôs (Rhos-on-Sea), in north Wales, is a chapel and holy well dedicated to St. Trillo. The well was discovered by the saint by miraculous agency. Trillo was a priest from the holy island of Bardsey, brother of St. Tegai and St. Llechid. His little chapel, that is almost invisible at the base of a low cliff on the foreshore, contains the well, that was found by the saint when he saw a Celtic cross of light appear, as a column, above the waters. Miraculously, curative fresh water was discovered on the shore, at a place where the salty waters of the Irish Sea should predominate. Today, St. Trillo's is still a place of votive prayer, where supplicants leave requests to God for healing and peace on scraps of paper that they leave on the altar. At Llandrillo yn Edernion, in Merionethshire, is another holy well of St. Trillo, resorted to for the relief of rheumatism.

ST. DYFNOG

Many Celtic saints are associated with springs that have been resorted to since ancient times by people seeking to be cured. St. Dyfnog, patron of the church of Llanrhaiadr, in Wales, is particularly associated with his holy well, Ffynnon Ddyfnog. The healing waters of this source were sanctified by the holy austerities practised by St. Dyfnog. Having sworn an oath of renunciation, the saint lived on bread and water alone, wearing a heavy horsehair shirt, held in place by an iron belt. His penance was to stand beneath the cold water of the holy spring as it poured over him. His virtues passed into the waters, and they have cured and healed ever since.

ST. ARTHMAEL

 t. Arthmael is a miraculous sixth century character. Like many of the Celtic saints, he lived at a time when it was possible to travel the land, preaching and doing good. Arthmael was Welsh, having been born in Glamorgan. He was from a religious family, being related to St. Cadfan, St. Maglorius, St. Malo, St. Padarn, St. Samson, and St. Tudno. He was also a member of St. Illtyd's "choir" of monks. He obtained rights from the Breton ruler to settle there, and it was in that land that he performed many miracles characteristic of Celtic saints in general.

Like St. George, St. Martha, St. Tudwal, and several other saints, Arthmael subdued a dragon that plagued the region around his monastery. He subdued it by tying his stole around its neck, and casting it into the river. In the valley of Loutéhel, the people had no water, so he struck the ground with his staff, and a spring of fresh water appeared. Like many saints associated with sources of water, St. Arthmael was noted for healing sick people. In the Middle Ages, he was prayed to by people with gout and rheumatism. Arthmael was one of the most popular saints in Brittany, and as the anglicized St. Ermyn, he was formerly revered in London at Westminster Abbey.

RIGHT: St. Arthmael shown in a stained glass window at St. Sauveur, Dinan.

ST. DWYNWEN

Like the earlier pagan gods and goddesses, there is a Celtic saint for each aspect of human existence. St. Dwynwen might be regarded as one of the most important, for she is the saint of true lovers. *The Myrvyrian Archaiology* describes her as the Welsh Venus. She was one of the numerous daughters of Brychan, king and saint. According to tradition, every faithful lover who prays to Dwynwen will either be cured of their love-passion, or gain union with his or her beloved. Her holy well in Anglesey, Ffynnon Ddwynwen, also called Crochan Llanddwyn (Llanddwyn's Cauldron), was resorted to by lovers requesting the resolution of their love affairs. Sadly, the well was destroyed in the nineteenth century. As the tutelary saint of lovers, she naturally inspired the poetry of the bards. Among the ancient Welsh saintly adages known as *The Sayings of the Wise*, is her watchword:

"Hast thou heard the saying of St. Dwynwen,
The Fair daughter of Brychan the Aged?
"There is none so lovable as the cheerful."

ᏬᏬ

The lovingness and compassion of St. Dwynwen were so great that she could even help lovers whose relationships were considered to be scandalous. Dafydd Llwyd of Mathafarn, who lived in the period 1395–1486, wrote that "Dwynwen will not hinder adultery." The celebrated medieval Welsh bard, Dafydd ap Gwilym, composed a cywydd that he then read to her image, requesting her to take the message to his lover, Morfudd:

"Dwynwen, beautiful as tears of frost,
In your candle-lit choir
Your golden statue knows well
How to soothe the pain and
torment of sad men.
He who keeps watch in radiant holiness
In your choir, shining Indeg,
Can never depart from Llanddwyn
With love-sickness nor a troubled mind."

ᏬᏬ

ABOVE: St. Dwynwen's holy well, Ffynnon Ddwynwen, in Anglesey, was visited by lovers seeking resolutions to their problems.

ST. GOVAN

St. Govan is best known as the hermit who lived at the place known as St. Govan's Head, where his chapel stands at the foot of cliffs enclosing a rocky inlet on the southern coast of Pembrokeshire, in southwest Wales. On the shore at St. Govan's is the saint's holy well, now dry, and blocked with a large stone. Fresh water springing on a salt water shore is a miraculous paradox that marks a place out as favored by the divine hand. The cliff nearby has pockets of red clay, that possess healing qualities. St. Govan, whom some have claimed to be the retired Arthurian knight, Gawain, spent the last part of his life by the shore there, warning passing ships of danger, and assisting survivors of shipwrecks. More probable than the Gawain identification however, is that St. Govan, whose other name was Mogopoc, was the disciple of the Irish bishop, St. Ailbe, who lived in the earlier part of the sixth century.

ABOVE: Gawain being refused entry to the Grail. Some have identified the Arthurian Knight with St. Govan.

According to local tradition the pirates, who then infested the seas around Pembrokeshire, hated Govan and tried to get rid of him. On one occasion, a band of freebooters landed and stole the silver bell that Govan used to call locals to prayer, and to warn passing ships of danger. They sailed away in triumph with the valuable bell, but they did not get far. Their ship was struck by a ferocious storm in view of the shore, and sank with all hands. But the bell was not lost, for a band of angels descended from above, into the sea and brought it out from the sunken wreck. So that it could never be stolen again, they embedded the bell within the rock at the back of the chapel. This is called Bell Rock.

On another occasion, pirates landed and attacked his meager settlement, but he backed into the cleft in Bell Rock. It is said that the rock closed around him and protected him until the pirates left. The cleft is large enough for a medium-sized person to squeeze into and inside it has ridges that resemble human ribs that are said to be the imprint of the saint. Once inside the cleft, one can hear the music of the spheres and may undergo uplifting out-of-body experiences.

ST. NECTAN

ABOVE: The waterfall at St. Nectan's Glen, near Tintagel, Cornwall. St. Nectan's bell is supposedly still heard here on occasion.

A somewhat comparable holy place exists close to Tintagel, in Cornwall, the reputed birthplace of King Arthur. There, St. Nectan built a cell above the Trevillitt River, where his waterfall, called St. Nectan's Kieve, emerges through a hole in the rock face. According to a current local legend, it is said that St. Nectan, like St. Govan, had a silver bell that hung in a tower behind his chapel. On his deathbed, believing that the Celtic church was in decline, he ordered that his bell should be thrown into the river, lest unbelievers should hear it ring. Like St. Govan's bell, it was taken out of the realm of humans. It is said that the bell still sounds occasionally, and that this is an ill omen to those who should hear it.

When St. Nectan died, two strange ladies appeared, and took possession of his chapel. They diverted the river, dug a grave beneath the waterfall, and buried Nectan's body in an oaken coffin, accompanied by his sacramental vessels and by other treasures. Then they allowed the river to resume its natural course over his remains. Similarly, King Alaric, the gothic despoiler of Rome, and King Offa of Mercia are both reputed to have received the same type of riverbed burial.

Although the name Nectan is a Pictish man's name, it is also a name given to water spirits, and there does seem to be a close relationship between the saint and ancient waterfall worship. After Nectan's death, the two women continued to live in his cell, but the place was considered to be desecrated as a result and the women were condemned as the source of all ills in the surrounding district.

CHAPTER XI

The Fall of the Celtic Church

Religious Rivalry

Although the progress of Christianity has often been portrayed as a triumphant series, composed of one success after the other, the real world was not like that. Even St. Patrick's conversion of Ireland was not as solid as he might have wished it to be. After his death, the new religion declined markedly, and the elder faith returned in many places. In the middle of the sixth century, the Irish high king, Ainmire, who reigned from 565 until 571, was so concerned at the decline of Christian practice and learning that he summoned St. Gildas from Wales to organize a revival. Gildas organized a supply of priests to be sent to Ireland from the Welsh monastic centres of Llancarfan and Menevia (St. David's). The monks chosen to re-

ABOVE: Many knights took up monastic orders after a lifetime of battle, but the austere rule dictated by Celtic monasticism discouraged many.

Christianize Ireland included St. Aidan, who sided with the Christian king of Leinster, Brandubh, and served as official curser of his enemy at the Battle of Dunbolg, in the year 598. It is recorded that at one time, fifty British bishops came to Ireland to visit Aidan. Even if this is an exaggeration, it shows that the Celtic church in Britain came to the assistance of the Irish church in its hour of greatest need.

But even though the Celtic missionaries worked hard and spread their church throughout western and central Europe, the Celtic church was on the losing side of a power struggle with the centralized church of Rome. One of the reasons for this was Celtic monasticism. Monastic life, under the rules of St. Columba and St. Columbanus, was harsh and unremitting, and the monasticism of the Benedictine rule was more attractive to prospective monks. This was because Benedict's rule was much more humane than the strict asceticism demanded by Celtic rule. Also, unlike the independent Celtic monasteries, the Benedictines had a centralized command structure and so, gradually, the Benedictine rule ousted the stricter Columbanian rule in the Celtic-founded monasteries. In some places, the transition was more gradual, with an intermediate stage that used a hybrid rule, based partly on the Columbanian, and partly on the Benedictine.

The Synod of Whitby: The Triumph of St. Wilfrid

So, in Anglo-Saxon England, both churches came into competition for converts, status, land, and tithes. Celtic Christianity first came into direct confrontation with Roman Catholicism in the Anglian state of Northumbria and this is where it met its downfall. In the middle of the seventh century, the Northumbrian king, Oswiu, was a Celtic Christian, but his consort, Eanfled, was from Kent, and thus of the Roman Catholic faith. The conflict arose, not through doctrinal differences, but because the Celtic and the Catholic churches used different calendars. This meant that each church celebrated the movable feasts, including Easter, on different dates. Thus, within the Northumbrian court there were two Christian observances that clashed with one another. When the Celtic Christians were feasting at Eastertide, the Catholics were still fasting in their Lent. This was clearly a state of affairs which needed rectifying. Advised by her Catholic priest, Romanus, Queen Eanfled asked the king to do something about it. He did, and in the year 664, he summoned a church meeting, at the monastery of Steaneshalch (Whitby), now known as the Synod of Whitby. It was organized by the abbess of the double monastery of nuns and monks, St. Hilda.

The Celtic delegation to the synod was led by Colman, Abbot of Holy Island (Lindisfarne), while the Catholics were represented by the more eloquent Abbot Wilfrid, from Ripon. Other important churchmen there included Catholics, who had openly condemned the Celtic church as schismatic. The bishop of Essex, Cedd, served as translator between the Gaelic-speaking Celts, and the Germanic

St. Augustine's Mission

In the year that St. Columba died, 597, the Roman Catholic missionary, St. Augustine, arrived in England. His mission was to convert the Saxons and Angles. In general, the Anglo-Saxons were willing to accept Christ into their pantheon along with Woden, Tiwaz, Thunor, Wayland, and Frea. Of course, it was intended that this dual faith would only be the first phase, before the old gods were eliminated. This had been done with apparent success in many places in mainland Europe. But in Britain, there was a complication. In the north and west, there was already a Christian church that was not under the control of Rome and that had converted a significant number to its beliefs.

ABOVE: St. Hilda who organized the Synod of Whitby to resolve the clash between the two Christian Churches.

tongue of the Anglo-Saxons. King Oswiu presided over the gathering. According to the ancient principle, "as above, so below," he told the assembly that, as they all expected the same kingdom in heaven, they should have the same celebration of the divine mysteries on earth. It was up to the priests to rectify it. Oswiu knew, in advance, from his wife and her adviser, that there was no way that the Catholics would change to the Celtic calendar. So he began by asking Colman to justify the Celtic tradition. In true Celtic style, Colman replied that his Easter was customary, having been received from his elders, who had handed it on in a direct line that led back to St. John the Evangelist, who devised it in the first place. Countering the Celtic tradition, Wilfrid asserted that he had traveled all through Europe and the eastern Roman Empire, and that everyone, except the Celts, used the calculation for Easter that he did. In reality, Wilfrid had only been to Rome, but he gave the impression that he had traveled widely in Africa, Greece, and Asia Minor, in contrast to the insular Colman, who had never left the British Isles.

The old ethnic animosity between Saxon and Celt seems to have played a significant part in this too, for Wilfrid went on to call the Britons and Picts "accomplices in obstinacy," who stood against "the rest of the universe." Wilfrid went on to attack the very roots of Celtic spirituality. He said that St. Columba was not a true saint, because he did not follow Catholic practices, and that the Celtic church was a false edifice, built on the precepts of Columba, and not St. Peter. As St. Peter was the founder of the true church, he asserted, followers of St. Columba must be in error. Wilfrid's arguments were accepted by King

Oswiu, and the result of the synod was a defeat for Columban Christianity because the king decided to replace the usages of the Celtic church with Roman Catholic practice. Oswiu was swayed by the argument that he would not get into heaven unless he followed St. Peter, "unless, when I come to the gates of heaven, there will be no-one to open them, because it is my enemy that has the keys." So, on the grounds that St. Peter, rather than St. Columba, has the keys to heaven, the Celtic church was forced to give way to the Catholic. Those Celtic priests who would not accept the Roman way were expelled immediately from the Anglo-Saxon realms. From Lindisfarne, Colman, accompanied by the Scots and thirty Anglian monks, traveled to Scotland, carrying with them some of the bones of St. Aidan. In Scotland, the Celtic Church did not recognize the decision of the Synod of Whitby, but the Catholic church now had the upper hand in Britain, and it appeared that Celtic Christianity was in retreat.

The Decline of the Celtic Church

After the Synod of Whitby, in the year 670, a synod was convened at Autun. This made the Benedictine rule compulsory in all monasteries in France and decreed that Celtic rule should be abolished there. Thus, between them, the synods of Whitby and Autun marked the beginning of the end of the Celtic Church. First, the Celtic Church was suppressed in the realms of the English and Frankish kings. Later, Catholic influence spread northward into the kingdom of the Picts, where the high king, Nechtan IV mac Derile, formally adopted Catholicism in the year 710. In the year 717, he cleared out all the Celtic churchmen of Iona from his realms, and sent them back into the land of the Scots to the west.

However, despite the eradication of Celtic Christianity from England and Pictland, the Celtic Church continued to flourish in Scotland, Ireland, and Brittany. In the eighth century, in response to Catholic inroads, a reformed Celtic spiritual movement, called the Culdees, came into being. This movement had a lasting effect in Ireland and in Scotland, but it, too, was finally forced to succumb to the more powerful Catholic traditions. In Brittany, the Celtic church continued to exist until the year 818, when that land was conquered by the Frankish emperor, Louis the Pious. The triumphant Emperor was shocked when Matmonoc, the abbot of Landevennec, who wore the Celtic tonsure, told him that the Breton monks living there "followed the usages of the Scots and Irish." As a result of this news Louis immediately ordered that all monasteries in Brittany should abandon their Celtic usages, and adopt the rule of St. Benedict at once. The Celtic church continued in existence longest in areas of Scotland and Cornwall. In Scotland, it was not until the year 1069 that the Celtic church was officially abolished by King Malcolm Canmore, at his wife's suggestion. However, in remote areas, isolated groups of Scottish Celtic monks continued to practice their religion in secret until the fourteenth century. Similarly, in Cornwall, Celtic services were still being conducted well into the twelfth century. Although the religious tradition was suppressed, the parallel bardic tradition, that had absorbed large parts of the Celtic Christian lore, has continued unbroken and still exists in some places to the present day.

BRUNANBURGH

In the year 930, a British bard composed a prophetic poem, Armes Prydein, which told that the English would be expelled from Britain, and the old sovereignty of the Britons restored. Under the holy banner of St. David, the prophecy told, the British armies would triumph against the English under King Athelstan. Recently, Athelstan had overthrown the Norse rulers of Northumbria, conquered Cornwall, and crushed a rebellion, headed by the king of Gwynedd, Edwall Vael, thereby annexing the land between the Severn and Wye rivers. A Scottish rebellion had also been dealt with. But the new bardic prophecy, which circulated around Cornwall, Wales, Cumbria, Strathclyde, and the parts of Scotland where the old populations remained, was a potent message of renewal and restoration. In the year 937, inspired by what they believed to be divine power, the Celts, and their Norse and Danish allies, set up a military confederation that challenged Athelstan to fight, not just for his kingdom, but for the very presence of the English in England. An army was assembled by the confederation. Numbering perhaps 60,000 soldiers, it was composed of contingents from the Celtic lands of Cornwall, Cumbria, Strathclyde, Scotland, Wales, and Ireland, along with expeditionary forces from the Dublin vikings, reinforced by Norwegian and Danish units. In religious terms, the confederation army was composed of Celtic Christians and Scandinavian pagans.

Once the army was assembled, the confederation heralds chose the battlefield, and set it aside, marking it with white hazel posts. According to ancient custom, once a battlefield was enhazeled in this way, by the heralds, it was necessary for the challenged party to appear to fight on it within two weeks, or to forfeit the kingdom. Informed that the field was enhazeled, Athelstan gathered his forces together and marched to the ancient sanctuary of Beverley, in Yorkshire. There, the king exchanged his sword for the holy banner of St. John of Beverley, that he used as his battle standard. Then, led by the royal standard bearer, the English army traveled westward to the battlefield at Brunanburgh. Outnumbered by more than two to one by the forces of the confederation, the English army nevertheless fought with enormous courage, and won an outright victory. Among the defeated, only the Danish forces withdrew in good order, and escaped by sea. The remaining confederation forces were left in disarray and, as they fled the battlefield, were followed and cut

down by the English warriors. Five kings and seven earls were slain on the confederation side on that one day. Thus, in religious terms, the Catholic English broke the power of the remaining Celtic Christians and the pagan Norse, and the prophecy of Armes Prydein was proved to be false. Having defeated the Celts and their allies decisively, Athelstan took the title Rex Totius Britanniae or, "King of All Britain," and from that time on Celtic power was forever suppressed in Great Britain.

BELOW: Brunanburgh was the last great battle between Celtic and Catholic Christianity.

ST. HILDA

The hostess of the Synod of Whitby was St. Hilda, a remarkable woman born of noble parentage, who had been encouraged by St. Aidan to set up a monastery in Northumbria. She devised her own monastic rule and, in 657, was made abbess of a double monastery, in which both nuns and monks lived. Under Hilda's rule, the monastery of Whitby became a noted center of learning. Hilda was the patroness of artists of various disciplines, including the famous poet, Caedmon. Unfortunately, her creative monastic rule, permitted by the Celtic tradition, was suppressed when the Celtic faction was overruled at the Synod of Whitby, and Hilda's contribution to religion was lost.

ST. MALACHY

St. Malachy was one of the last Irish monks in the old Celtic tradition. Like Merlin and St. Columba, he left us a series of enigmatic prophecies. Born Maelmhaedhoc O'Morgair, in Armagh, in the year 1094, Malachy served under Imhar O'Hagan and eventually became abbot of the monastery of Armagh, then bishop of Connor, and finally archbishop. Malachy was recognized as being gifted with the power of prophecy, even foretelling the day and hour of his own death in the year 1148. During a pilgrimage to Rome in 1139–40, Malachy experienced a series of visions in which the future popes of Rome were told to him. They were described as a series of consecutive Latin epithets, that supposedly described the character of each of the popes-to-be for centuries into the future until the Last Judgment. Some of these epithets are beautiful and spiritual, such as Lilium et Rosa, "The lily and the rose," supposedly Pope Urban VIII, Flores Circumdati, "Surrounded with flowers," equated with Pope Clement XI, others are matter of fact, such as Vir Religiosus, "A religious man," Pope Pius VIII; while others are mystically symbolic, like Axis in Medietate Signi, "An axis in the middle of the sign," Pope Sixtus V. But not all of the epithets are so flattering. Malachy prophesied popes with the character of Canis et Coluber, "A dog and a serpent," Pope Leo XII; Aquila Rapax, "The rapacious eagle," Pope Pius VII; or Bellua Insatialibis, "The insatiable beast," Pope Innocent XI. In all, Malachy mentions 112 popes, ending with Pope Petrus Romanus, "Peter the Roman." "In the last persecution of the Holy Church of Rome," concludes Malachy, "Peter the Roman will reign, who will feed his flock amidst many troubles; after which the seven-hilled city will be destroyed, and the Terrible Judge will judge the people."

ABOVE: The decorative arts flourished under St. Hilda's enlightened guidance.

LEFT: St. Hilda, who set up her own creative monastery in Northumbria, is shown here at Hartlepool.

ABOVE: A vision of the ancient Celtic seers, druids, and poets, known as the *aos dana*, or gifted people.

Celtic Relics
from the Age of Saints

The Destruction of Piety

During the Reformation, protestants condemned, as objects of superstition and idolatry, every thing and every place formerly venerated by Roman Catholics. Many of the traditions of the Celtic saints, that had survived in Catholic ritual and custom, were forcibly terminated. In this time, the Celtic spiritual legacy was seriously challenged. In addition to prohibiting traditional rites and ceremonies, they actively destroyed as much as they could of the holy artefacts of the saints. Puritan Protestant zealots took it as their God given duty to eliminate every "idolatrous image" at which Catholic "superstition" could take place. So, in an orgy of destruction, they pulled down, smashed, and burned the church's holy images of Christ, Our Lady, and the saints, smashed Celtic crosses, broke down altars, shattered stained glass windows, and dug up the tombs of saints and threw their bones onto garbage dumps. In a short time, a thousand years of piety was extirpated.

The tradition of venerating Christian relics had been brought to Britain in the fifth century. The veneration of the bones of saints, preserved in special tombs, was only part of the tradition smashed at the Reformation. Other objects that had belonged to saints – books, sticks, bells, crosses, and other personal effects – had been preserved, and used as magical objects in times of need. These relics of the Celtic saints were kept originally by relatives of the saint, and later by descendant families that served, through the generations, as hereditary keepers, known as *maer*, *dewar*, or *coarb*. None of the Celtic saintly relics were ever actually the property of any church. Although they may have been kept at

abbeys and churches, they remained the property of the family of whom the original owner was ancestor. Wherever the family has not died out, or given up its ownership, hereditary keepers remain. Traditionally, the keeper received a small salary, generated by ancestral land, that legally belonged to the holy object itself, and could not be sold. As payment for carrying out the duties of relic keeping, the keeper was paid the income generated by the land. Thus, the family, the holy object, and the land were kept together and perpetuated through successive generations.

ABOVE: The richly jeweled cover of a copy of the gospels, believed to have belonged to St. Molaise.

ST. PATRICK, ST. LACHTIN AND ST. COLUMBA

Almost miraculously, a number of precious, holy relics have survived the destructiveness of time, and have come down to the present day, because generations of family keepers have preserved them from destruction, for more than a millenium. Even some of the skeletal relics of saints are still in existence, among them the shrines containing the armbones of St. Patrick and St. Lachtin. Formerly, there were numerous bony relics of saints preserved all over the Celtic realms, but most

ABOVE: The Grave of St. Patrick,
Downpatrick, Co. Down, Ireland.

suffered destruction at the hands of reformers. Other relics of saints, mainly their possessions, are more plentiful. Like the bones, they were enclosed in costly reliquaries of precious metal, richly ornamented with Celtic artwork and sometimes bejeweled. Among them, the *cathach* of St. Columba is one of the most remarkable relics that has survived until the present day. It is a prayer book, reputed to have been written by the saint himself. For centuries, inside its protective casket, it was preserved by its current hereditary keeper, who was a member of the O'Donnells, successors of the northern Uí

Neill tribe, of Ulster, of which St. Columba was a member. The texts, written by the great Celtic saint, were considered to have great power, so they were used in apotropaic rituals, believed to turn aside evil times of trouble. In 1497, for example, before a battle, the *cathach* was carried by its hereditary keeper, three times sunwise around the O'Donnell army.

According to Manus O'Donnell, writing in the sixteenth century, it was "the main relic of St. Columbkille in the land of the Cinel Conaill Gulban. It is contained within a silver-gilt box which must never be opened. And every time it has been carried round the army before a battle, turning to the right, three times, the army returned victorious."

In 1691, after the defeat of the Catholic forces in Ireland, the remnant of the army escaped to France, and the *cathach* was taken there by the O'Donnell keeper. It was brought back to Ireland, in 1802, by Sir Neal O'Donnell, and the tattered ancient book was removed from the casket. Later scholars have dated it to the middle of the seventh century, so it is possible that it is indeed Columba's own book.

S.COLVMBA   S.PATRICIVS

ABOVE: After dangerous adventures in Ireland, St. Columba emigrated to the holy island of Iona, west of Scotland, which became one of the most important centers of Christian learning in northern Europe.

ABOVE: With his holy Staff of Jesus, St. Patrick expelled all the demons and snakes from Ireland, transforming Erin into a haven of holiness.

HOLY STAVES, CROZIERS, AND BELLS

Because of their fragility, books are rare relics. Wooden and metal objects are sturdier, and so have a better chance of surviving the vagaries of time. One of the attributes of the Celtic saint was his pastoral staff, and a number of these have survived. Being holy objects, they were often encased in rich metal coatings that protected them against destruction. The croziers of St. Mel and St. Dympna, the crozier of the abbots of Clonmacnois, and the Lismore crozier all still exist, encased in fine metalwork. All of these have passed from their hereditary keeper's families into museums. The pastoral staff of St. Moluaig, of the Island of Lismore, however, is a thornwood stick in the possession of the Livingstone family, hereditary dewars of the parish.

LEFT: St. Augustine holding his pastoral staff. A number of similar staffs still survive today.

Even more durable than their pastoral staves are the saints' bells. Hammered from sheet metal, rather than cast, the bells used by Celtic saints are divine instruments of sacred power. Following the Egyptian custom, the Celtic saints used bells to drive away any mischievous, or evil, spirits.

ABOVE: The beautifully decorated shrine which holds St. Patrick's bell.

The Arthurian *Perlesvaus* recounts how evil spirits were overcome by the divine sound of a holy bell. In his *Miscellanies*, the seventeenth century antiquary, John Aubrey, commented that in his time, "the curious do say that the ringing of bells exceedingly disturbs spirits." The saints' bells were also used to summon the faithful to prayer. Solemn oaths were sworn on bells, and they could also empower curses and exorcisms. When someone was dying, the sound of the bell helped the soul to depart in peace, by protecting it from the demons that attempted to carry it off to the infernal regions. This is the origin of the "passing bell" still tolled at Christian funerals.

Most surviving Celtic saints' relics are no longer protected by hereditary keepers. Over the years, museums have acquired them, as treasures of national heritage. Perhaps the most significant is *Clog-an-Eadbacta Phatraic* "the Bell of St. Patrick's Will." Used by the apostle of Ireland during his lifetime, it was originally buried with St. Patrick, but after sixty years in the grave, it was dug up. Then, the O'Mellan family was appointed as its keeper, and they protected it until 1441. Subsequently, it was passed from owner to owner until it came into the possession of the state. Now, it is on view in the National Museum in Dublin, rightly honored as a national treasure. A comparable Scottish saintly bell is the Skellat, preserved in the Municipal Museum at Dumbarton. The majority of Celtic saints' bells still in existence in Ireland, Scotland, Wales, France, Germany, and Switzerland are now in museums. There are however, notable exceptions. The bell of St. Cumasnach is preserved by its hereditary keepers at Roscommon, Ireland; St. Eunan's is kept in the church of Tom Eunan, at Kincraig, in Scotland; and the bell of St. Gwynhoedl is to be found at Llangwnnadl church, in Wales.

We are fortunate that we still have so many links with the age of the Celtic saints. But, for every surviving holy relic, there must have been hundreds, if not thousands, that have been lost or destroyed.

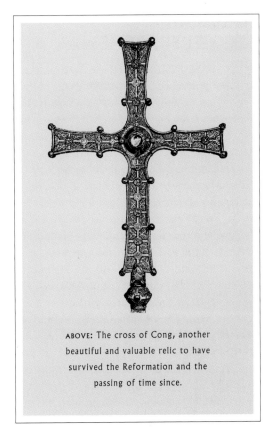

ABOVE: The cross of Cong, another beautiful and valuable relic to have survived the Reformation and the passing of time since.

Many fantastic relics, described by ancient authors, are no longer with us today. For instance, Giraldus Cambrensis tells us that in the twelfth century, at St. Harmon's Church, in the sea of Llangurig, in Radnor, east Wales, was "The staff of St. Curig, covered on all sides with gold and silver and representing in its upper part the form of a cross." Miraculous powers of healing were ascribed to this particular cross, especially in the case of people afflicted with glandular disorders. But during the Reformation, like so many other holy things, it was taken away by the commissioners and burned.

LEFT: A crozier found in Cormac's chapel, Cashel. Being made of copper, only the head has survived.

POSTSCRIPT
THE CELTIC RENEWAL

The Reformation saw the destruction of many of the relics of the Celtic saints, and it might have seemed then that the old ways of Celtic spirituality were at an end. However, certain elements of Celtic tradition did not die, and were maintained in local customs and traditions. But the rediscovery of Celtic religion was long and slow. In Wales, in the eighteenth century, following the rediscovery of some ancient texts, there arose an renewed national awareness of the Druidic heritage. This resulted in the publication of several influential books, and the renewal of the cultural traditions of the Eisteddfod, the annual gathering of the bards.

After being ignored for a long time, the old traditions of the Druids and bards were gradually reexamined. Those who studied ancient Celtic culture realized that the old traditions were not harmful, but contained a benign awareness of humans' harmony with nature. The Druid John Toland's influential book *Christianity not Mysterious*, took the Pelagian view, denying the necessity for revelation, and later William Blake wrote "The antiquities of every Nation under Heaven is no less sacred than that of the Jews. They are the same thing." Through these inspired bards, the ancient Celtic awareness of the immanence of God in nature, the presence of the divine in all things, had returned to learned society.

In Ireland, the recognition that Celtic spirituality was of value coincided with the re-awakening of national awareness. Numerous ancient texts were published, and the special nature of the Celtic saints was acknowledged. Parallel with this renewal of Welsh and Irish tradition, startling things were emerging from Scotland. During his travels in the Scottish Highlands, the Reverend Alexander Carmichael came into contact with the rich bardic oral tradition of the people there. Until Carmichael took an interest, Scottish academics and clergymen had been unaware of the rich heritage of the crofters and fisherfolk of their country. Carmichael collected a large number of Gaelic prayers and sayings that startled the learned with their remarkable Celtic imagery. Published in *Carmina Gadelica*, they attest to a continued tradition of Celtic spirituality, containing much derived from the Celtic church, suppressed so many centuries earlier. Today, Celtic spirituality is no longer the property of a bygone era. It is a living force in the contemporary world. The spiritual legacy of the Celtic saints is now recognized as one of the more valuable currents of the European tradition. This is apparent anywhere that spiritual people meet. The prayers and sayings of the Celtic saints are readily available in many languages, while their holy places are visited by increasing numbers of pilgrims.

The twentieth century has seen wars of unprecedented scale and ferocity. They have disrupted traditional ways of life and thought, bringing a crisis of faith, in both human and divine powers. Technological progress has also brought spiritual chaos and the destruction of the environment. Here, we can sense a parallel with the age of the Celtic saints who, in an era of social and spiritual breakdown, held on to their principles and gave people spiritual stability in an age of chaos.

RIGHT: During his travels in the Scottish Highlands, Carmichael collected prayers and sayings full of Celtic imagery.

CHRONOLOGY OF THE CELTIC SAINTS

(some dates are, by necessity, approximate)

CAW	*fourth century*
COEL HÊN	*fourth century*
NINIAN	*fourth century*
HELEN	*fourth century*
PELAGIUS	*dec. 430*
FINGAR	*dec. 455*
PATRICK	390–461
CIARAN	446–530
ILLTYD	450–525
DYFRIG	450–546
DOGED FRENIN	*fifth century*
GWEN TEIRBRON	*fifth century*
HOIERNIN	*fifth century*
DWYNWEN	*fifth–sixth centuries*
NON	*fifth–sixth centuries*
PABO	*fifth–sixth centuries*
AILBE	*early sixth century*
BEUNO	*sixth century*
COLLEN	*sixth century*
DYFNOG	*sixth century*
ENDELIENTA	*sixth century*
GWYNLLYW	*sixth century*
NECTAN	*sixth century*
SEIRIOL	*sixth century*
TRILLO	*sixth century*
TYDECHO	*sixth century*
BRIGID OF KILDARE	*dec. 525*
FINNIAN	*dec. 549*
SAMSON	485–565
BRENDAN	486–575